THE INCREDIBLE
FATHER

THE INCREDIBLE FATHER

Jagi Aisa Baap Vhava

DR. MURHARI KELE

Translated from Marathi by
Dr.Dnyaneshwar Suryawanshi

PARTRIDGE
A Penguin Random House Company

Print information available on the last page.

To order additional copies of this book, contact
Partridge India
000 800 10062 62
orders.india@partridgepublishing.com

www.partridgepublishing.com/india

CONTENTS

About author: Dr. Murhari S. Kele is a Chief Engineer at Maharashtra State Electricity Distribution Company Ltd. He is posted at the Company's headquarter 'Prakashgad' in Mumbai. He has authored many books.

About translator: Dr. Dnyaneshwar P. Suryawanshi is Assistant Professor and Head, Department of English at Vivekanand Arts, Sardar Dalipsingh Science and Commerce College, Aurangabad.

To my diligent Mother, Who was as hard as coconut shell outwardly, but as sweet and pure as its water from within......

TRANSLATOR'S NOTE

It was an amazing moment when I first saw '*Jagi Aisa Baap Vhava*,' a biography originally written in Marathi by Dr. Murhari Kele. The cover page was stunningly gripping which made it clear that the book was the biography of the biographer's father.

There are some reasons why I chose to translate this book. The first is more important as there is a close similarity between father in the book and my father. I found this book immensely compelling as it puts forward the life of a *Warkari* and a *kirtankar* which is much similar to my father's. I have translated this biography because there is considerable similarity between my father and the biographer's father Sopankaka Kele, the subject of this biography. I have translated the present book also because I am emotionally attached to the *Warkari* sect and Marathi saint poetry since my childhood. There is one more reason why I decided to undertake this task. On behalf of Dr. Kele, my friend Dr. Mahesh Kharat requested me to do the translation. Finally, I consented to shoulder the assignment. I feel quite happy now to put my translation before readers.

It proved to be a difficult venture to translate the Marathi book as it has so many untranslatable words and expressions belonging to the *Warkari* sect. The list includes *Wari, Warkari, dindi, gatha, Haribhakt Paraayan, kirtan, jagar, Kakda, Mauli, gopichandan, bukka, hadpi* and so on. The connotative implication of these words is completely indigenous having cultural and spiritual strands. As a result, I have retained all these words so as to keep their beauty and cultural undercurrents intact. I did not want to 'lose this book' in translation. Therefore, I decided to include such words in the translated text. The original book comprises many lines from *the Dnyaneshwari* and *abhangas* of some Marathi saint poets. There lies profound beauty in this saint literature. It took some months to translate these poetic lines. I have rendered and rephrased the rendering of this poetry for innumerable times. Despite these repeated efforts, I could not get complete satisfaction. I have made an attempt to translate this Marathi poetry into English by following a crude pattern of rhyme and without proper metrical pattern. I feel that it is highly impossible to transport the ethos of Marathi saint poetry into English following the rigid norms of rhyme and metre. I know that this translation has many limitations as this is my maiden endeavour. However, I have sincerely tried to do justice to prose and poetry from the book. It is up to readers to justify the merit of this translation.

It's the matter of sheer pleasure to thank some people who have helped shaping the translation. I have no words to thank Dr. Murhari Kele and Dr. Mahesh Kharat who discovered a translator in me. How can I thank my father? My father helped me in explicating varied meanings of *abhangas* and lines from *the Dnyaneshwari*. Without this contribution, this work would not have reached its conclusion. I am thankful to my friend Rajkranti Walse for being the first reader of the draft. Dr. Santosh Karwande, Dr. Ajay Deshmukh and Shridhar Nandedkar deserve a load of thanks for their significant suggestions. I am indebted to my friends Adv. Hanmant Patil, Anil Dabhade, Nitin Kendre, Ketan Sapkal and Vishnu Bhagile for their all time help. I thank all the members in my family for their patient support and understanding. Finally, am grateful to all those who directly or indirectly furthered this translation.

Dr.Dnyaneshwar Suryawanshi

FOREWORD

Sacred is that land and divine race,
Where Hari's disciples are born with His grace.

That lineage and country become sacred where saints are born. It is because saints are holy from birth to birth. A sage is born in a family because of his ancestors' austerities.

Maharashtra is the reverent land of saints. There have been so many people on the path of divinity which is shown by saints through their writings. Sopankaka, the subject of present writing, was one of such people. His transformation from commoner Sopanya to much dignified Sopankaka Kele Maharaj was quite amazing.

We all have respect and affection for our parents. However, my life is illuminated as I had respectful father like Kaka. I received his love and blessings because he was my father and guru as well. A father is bound to have so many responsibilities. Every father nourishes his children, gives them proper education and inculcates values in them. Yet Kaka's fatherhood was very different as he cared for the society as if a parent and has shown people the path of goodness by elevating them spiritually and instilling divine values in them.

> *You Saints are my parents benign;*
> *How would I, a fallen describe you fine.*

Quite alike the above expressions by Saint Tukaram, very few people are fortunate to have a saint as their 'guru' and a parent. I am one of such people. Respected Kaka was a guru, father and everything for me.

In one of his *abhangas*, Saint Tukaram says that master's service, guru's devotion, keeping of father's promises and husband's services are equal to the worship of Lord Vishnu. Expectations of that person get fulfilled who speaks truth and becomes unhappy by witnessing others' sorrow.

It was Yedshi where spiritual values were ingrained in Kaka. On the basis of this treasure, he expanded the orchard of devotion. He de-addicted people and made them true devotees of Lord Vitthal. Throughout his life, Kaka preferred divine truth over worldly engagements, the other over the self, humility over pride, action over popularity and liberation over living. As a result, he attained *moksha*.

Kaka faced intense poverty and was completely illiterate. He was from such a social background where ignorance was prevalent. Despite his rural farming background lacking divine touch, Kaka achieved divinity. His accomplishments are nothing but divine grace.

We could not notice how Kaka reached divinity by the company of some great devotees, by their thinking, by his own study and tenacity.

We could not notice how Kaka journeyed from illiteracy to literacy, from a commoner Sopan to venerated Sopankaka, from Sopankaka to dedicated devotee of his Lord, and from such a devotee to the God's votary attaining godliness. His accomplishments resulted from the company of some enlightened devotees, their thoughts, his learning as well as his resolve. I am writing this not because he was my father, and I loved him. People who have closely observed and experienced him will tell the same story I am telling.

Kaka would never mention his close relations with various notable personalities and his discussion with them, his divine experiences and his association with Lord Hanuman. He believed that expressions of these kinds harm their power. Considering all these matters, it can be stated that

May there be a father very ace,
Whose clan attains divine grace?

I was mostly out of village for my education and later due to the job. Whenever I came to village, Kaka and I used to have discussion on spiritual matters. It was the usual matter to discuss the topic of revered Yedshikar brothers Ramkrishnabhau and Bhagwanbhau. Besides, the name of Yedshikar brothers' teacher Bapu Master would also be mentioned in the course of discussion. Moreover, Kaka would cite the name of much esteemed Rangnath Maharaj Parbhanikar.

The present writing is based on a variety of sources. They include Kaka's memories, incidents told by people including my mother Nani, my sisters, relatives, Kaka's disciples and people from Kelewadi. Additionally, the written records of my cousin Dattuappa Kele, Kaka's notebooks and the incidents which I actually witnessed have helped the formation of this book. I have no words to thank all these people for their contribution.

I am grateful to Dattuappa Kele, my friend Suresh Londhe, Bharat and Bajirao Chothave, Manoharbuwa Gosavi and Arunojirao Deshmukh for insisting me to include their memories concerning Kaka. The contribution of prominent poet Loknath Yashwant is quite phenomenal. More importantly, heartfelt thanks to my wife Mrs. Manisha, my lovely children Ajinkya, Vivek and Sanskruti who never grumbled as I spent much of my time on the book. I thank them for understanding and encouraging me.

Finally, I am thankful to all those who directly or indirectly helped shaping the book.

Kaka always shied away from publicity because he never inclined to be popular. He suggested his humility by calling himself a trifling and mere dust on saints' feet.

I conclude my foreword and request readers in the words of Dnyaneshwar Mauli:

You add to it if anything needed;
Remove my words if they are weeded.
With these words I pray you all,
Accept me as your brother small.

THE BLESSINGS...

So many blessings to Mr. Murhari Sopankaka Kele.

I have gone through your reverential father's biography which you have written. The incidents given in the book, your father's hardworking nature, his feelings and thoughts towards the individual and society, etc. are boundlessly enlightening. Language of the biography is very lucid and fluid explicating various incidents in Kaka's life. Whoever reading this book will come across Kaka's diligence, ready-wittedness and taciturn nature giving an appropriate lesson through a small but suggestive virtuous conduct. This behaviour is quite imitative for ordinary people.

Kaka lived such a life which involved financial difficulties and appropriation of money earned through valid means. He never became prey to the temptations of money. His way of life was based on the foundation of upright action. This biography is an ideal and inspirational reading which gives us a glimpse of Kaka's candid, ethical and unfailingly benevolent disposition.

It's a matter of sheer pleasure and pride that Murhari has penned his father's 'biography.' We, including Murhari's father, some devotees, some *kirtankars* and *talkaris* had been on the pilgrimage to some holy places. At that time, we had witnessed Murhari's father's modest and endowed life. Besides, this biography can aptly be described as the father's 'factual biography.' It is because the biographer neither exaggerates nor belittles the facts. The writing of this biography is flawless and, as a result, it deserves to be fittingly termed as a biography. The present book is quite exemplary to that person who wishes to understand implications behind the word 'biography.' This biography is not *the Vedas*' methodical treatise or a theory book. It is the record of a person's moral fibre and ideals he promoted throughout his life. This book minutely details how human life reaches completion by becoming well versed in *the Vedas*, by being devoted to *the Brahma,* by being compassionate and by one's submission to guru. These achievements are attained through high character and endowed life which involve rationality, renunciation, emancipation and triumph over material desires. This book neither tells the theory formed by justice nor spiritual philosophy. However, Murhari's writing of his father's 'biography' proves that a layman can become an excellent *pravachankar* and *kirtankar* by good and right conduct, good company and listening to and reading of good books.

In this book, we come across the mention of Late Rangnath Maharaj Parbhanikar, Late Bankatswami, Late Dnyaneshwar Mauli Chakarwadikar and Late Tatyasaheb Kore alias Tatyasaheb Waskar. Besides, there are references to Kaka's association with *kirtankars* including Late Manoharbuwa Gosavi, Late Krushnadas Lohia Maharaj, Late

Ramkrishnabhau Yedshikar, Late Bhagwanbhau Yedshikar and with others. I have been closely related to all these people except Bankatswami. It is because from 1950 to 1965, I stayed at Pandharpur in Alibagkar Maharaj's *math* during *Chaturmas*.

In its sixth chapter, the biography comprises my opinion about Murhari's father. Sandalwood does not need any proclamation about its smell. In the same way good people do not need any propaganda about their inherent qualities.

As per domains, the nature of God is three-fold. In terms of thinking, 'God' is indefinable, formless, beyond attributes, rejoicing, far and wide, perpetual and consistent. In emotional sphere, 'God' is set to have six attributes: success, riches, generosity, knowledge, renunciation and opulence. He is 'God' because of these qualities. Finally, in the field of behavior, 'God' is equal to virtuous actions. It means He is exactly a parallel to good and right behaviour. Similar to this way of thoughts, the nature of God for Sopankaka was his upright conduct throughout his life.

Mr. Murhari Kele is a senior officer working in M. S. E. D. C. L. which is a power distribution company of Maharashtra. The credit of his today's worldly and divine accomplishments goes to his father himself. I wish his life, like his father's, get enriched by virtuous behavior and wisdom to lead him towards the fruitfulness of life.

Haribhakt Paraayan **Dr. Kisan Maharaj Sakhare,
'Sadhakashram', Alandi (Devachi), Pune**. (M.S.)

CHAPTER 1

A Gem in Dust

There is a poem in English. It says that,

> *"Some pearls are dazzling, lustrous and genuine.*
> *They get valued when people spot them.*
> *However, such pearls do not catch people's*
> *sight and therefore remain unvalued.*
> *It is because they lay at the bottom of the*
> *sea in a cave, dark and fathomless."*

Some flowers are abundantly fragrant. Had they blossomed in a garden, connoisseurs would have appreciated them. Some of them would have put the flowers in theirs plaits, some on their coats and some would have composed poems on them. But these appealing flowers blossom in a desolate desert from where their fragrance is

1

aimlessly transported by the wind. Similar are some people like my father. He was a gem concealed in dust.

There is a tiny village namely Kelewadi on a plateau in Washi tehsil of Osmanabad district in Maharashtra. Approximately hundred and fifty people reside in the village of forty to fifty houses. The village is attached to the Washi Grampanchayat. As a result, Kelewadi is far away from development. It has no shops and lacks state transport bus facility.

It was the time approximately one hundred years ago. The footprints of the bygone period are seen even today. There was a huge banyan tree. The wreckage of the dilapidated houses is still found. A quick glance at the village may give us an idea that it's a place of forty to fifty houses.

Aabaji belonged to *Dhangar* community whose family God was Khandoba. His forefathers basically hailed from Mangrul in Solapur district. He migrated to Bhoom tehsil for some reasons. Afterwards, his surname was changed to 'Kele.' Our kinsmen are residing at Mangrul until now. Aabaji Panduji Kele and his wife Lakshmibai were from a labourer family from Kelewadi. Since most of the people's surname was Kele, the village was also named as Kelewadi. It is said that our old surname was 'Pandhare.' Some elderly people tell an amusing story about how 'Pandhare' became 'Kele': Some people were invited for a meal. It was the time when people used to get plenty of dairy products. There was no scarcity of even ghee. People used to keep dairy products such as milk, curd, ghee, etc. in earthenware called 'keli.' It was a type of earthen pot used for the purpose. As they were from *Dhangar* community, people were naïve and simple. They served ghee to the invited people by *keli* as if it was water. As a result, our forefathers were being chided by using the term 'Kelya' and our village was baptized as 'Kelewadi.' Following this legend, we got our surname 'Kele.' Much later we came to know that our family God was Khandoba from Shegud.

There had been the nuisance of mice and rats in our village which spoiled grains to a great extent. Hence people decided to shift their residences by the lower side of the plateau near their farm. Consequently, all the people from *Dhangar* community stayed in the upper *wadi* and remaining Maratha people in the lower, near their fields. At present, people from the old village have started constructing houses in new Kelewadi.

The habitation namely Kelewadi is at the distance of 6-7 kilometers from Washi which was erstwhile in Bhoom tehsil of Osmanabad district. This place belongs to the Marathwada region of Maharashtra. The region is considered to be a backward area. Now Washi is a *taluka* and Kelewadi is divided into two parts, Upper and Lower Kelewadi.

How much prosperous may be the life of a *Dhangar?* Nevertheless, he made his life contented by hard work. This was my grandfather Aabaji who had six children, four sons and two daughters. They were Namdev, Muktabai, Bhanudas, Sopan, Tanibai and Sambhaji. It is quite clear by these names that there was a great influence of *Warkari* sect on the family.

Actually the conditions of *Dhangar* community, its culture, its overall surrounding and customs were not that much favorable for the pious and gentle line of thoughts advocated by the *Warkari* sect. Until now, this community is not thought to be reputed and cultured. Furthermore, it is away from urban way of life and its family God is Khandoba. There had been the practice of rooster sacrifice before a Goddess. I remember there is a temple of village deity even today on the plateau. We called that deity 'Satwai.' As children, we were afraid of the deity. Our fear was the result of the sacrifice before the deity. The sight of sacrifice was quite stunning and cruel which made our tender minds tremor. There is a large banyan tree even today. The remains of the houses made of stones and mud are still witnessed. The temple was equally dreadful for us. Near the temple there were extremely deep gorge and cliffs of pitch black rocks which left people unnerved. It was the place where our forefathers dwelt and my father was born.

It was much neglected *Dhangar* community in which customs of animal sacrifice to the deities were predominant. In this ritualistic society and hustle and bustle, the gem namely Sopan was born to Aabaji.

Kaka's Childhood

My grandparents Aabaji Panduji Kele and Lakshmibai had six children. The eldest son Namdev was called by the title Dada. Mukta was the second issue and the eldest daughter. The third issue was Bhanudas who was called as Bapu. The fourth child, the subject of our biography, was Sopan who was known as Kaka. He might have born around 1920. Since Kaka's parents were illiterate and there hadn't been any schools in rural area, it is difficult to mention the exact date of his birth. The fifth issue was Tanibai followed by Sambhaji whom all called Anna. It was a joint family in which Kaka was younger than his brothers Namdev and Bhanudas. Both of them were married. Bhanudas was living in Savargaon with his wife Parubai. It was the place of Parubai's parents where Bhanudas was dwelling with his in-laws. We, rest of the members were a joint family. My mother Nani's parents belonged to Kelewadi itself, and therefore, she mostly stayed

4

with her parents. Sambhaji was Kaka's younger brother and my youngest uncle.

It was the time when Marathwada belonged to the Hyderabad state ruled by Nizam. The Nizam's private militia Razakars had his patronage that oppressed people. It was the time of utmost financial difficulty for our family. Dada and Bapu had sought some menial employment. They were the bread-winners of the family. Dada got married when Kaka was still a child. There was a custom in our community to sacrifice nine male goats at the time of marriage. Kelewadi was a small village having only one hundred and fifty residents. When Bapu got married, there had been two more marriages in our village. Total twenty seven male goats were put to death on the occasion. As the village was very small, all the meat was not finished off. Therefore, small children were found carrying the dried meat in their pockets and eating it while wandering through fields. Even Kaka was among these children. It was told that he was 'haunted' by a ghost while roaming through hills. For a long period, he remained in that senseless state. He was brought home and locked in a room. However, it was told that the locked door would automatically unlock and unlatch. Afterwards, Kaka chose to sleep in hills and vales as usual.

Meanwhile Dada and Bapu fell ill. Both of them were the working members in the family. Since there were no hospitals at that time, patients were taken to an exorcist. At the distance of fifty kilometers from our village, there is a shrine of 'Bajibaba' in Beed district. There was not transportation facility like today. Aabaji, my grandfather, used to take the patients to Bajibaba in a bullock cart on every Thursday. They were tired of visiting the place regularly for six months, but malaria did not give the patients any respite. On the other hand, people began calling Kaka 'mad' as he was 'haunted' by ghost. The expenses on marriage, two ailing sons and a mad son altogether proved to be quite distressing to Aaba. After a year, the two sickly sons recovered from their illness. Both of them sought labour with Deshmukhs on yearly basis. Bapu got a whole piece of cloth from his earnings. From this cloth he made dhotis, shirts and turbans for all and assured sustenance to the family for that year. Meanwhile Kaka's appetite was affected by his strange disposition. It was the matter of lot of apprehension. It was said that a ghost let Saint Ramdas Swami meet his guru who directed him to his destination. Even in Kaka's case, the 'ghost' proved to be benevolent. He took Kaka to Ballav Rishi and made him do the reading of the Holy Scripture *the Navnath*.

It was very difficult to get a person for reading such scriptures. There was a person namely Dattu Mulay in nearby village Kanheri. He twice read *the Navnath*. It can be stated that Kaka got rid of his affliction by these readings and even by his devotion to Ballav Rishi.

Kaka obtained employment of grazing goats with a local Deshmukh on the yearly basis. Even Dattu Mulay from Kanheri served there. The Deshmukh was highly regarded by the people of Kelewadi and Kanheri. Every dispute from these villages was settled by the Deshmukh and there was no scope for police cases. Even the simple matter like partition of land between brothers was resolved in the house of Deshmukh. His decision was always final. His awe was such that nobody dared to defy his judgement. There was a room in his mansion where erring people were locked. When the mistake was grave the offender was either whipped or caned. People from both the villages generally avoided wrongdoing and were happily living together. For five years, Kaka did the work of grazing goats with the Deshmukh. Kaka's health improved as he consumed a lot of milk.

By this time, Kaka's age might be eighteen to twenty. He was not able to get married though he had crossed his marriageable age. As a result, my grandmother used to call him ill fated since there was the practice of child marriage. Nani, my mother, told that she was eight or nine when her marriage with Kaka took place in old Kelewadi itself. She was born around 1931. Her parents had eleven children of which Sonabai, my mother, was the fourth. Parents from both sides belonged to the same village. It was customary to give dowry to the parents of the bride instead to those of groom's. The dowry of four hundred rupees, the cost of clothes and expenses of the wedding were borne by Kaka's parents. Finally, Kaka was wedded to Sonabai, the daughter of Santram Bodke. The ritualistic wedding took place in the old village.

Although there was the practice of child marriage, the bride was not immediately sent to live with her husband and in-laws. Therefore, six to seven years following her marriage, Nani stayed with her parents up to the age of sixteen. In the meantime, both the families, of course, were in each other's access. As these families were large in size, there had been frequent and mutual resorting. Kaka's elder brothers too were married and all of them had a joint family. My uncle Bhanudas and his wife Parubai were living in Savargaon and rest of the family was in Kelewadi.

Kaka never felt at home in worldly life though he was married. His worldly business hadn't begun yet. Moreover, my mother was still staying with her parents. Although Kaka was the caretaker of the livestock, his mind was somewhere else while grazing goats and sheep. It means that always he had longing for God. He would dip into the nearby pond whenever he felt uncomfortable. There is a shrine of Ballav Rishi close to our farm. Kaka was obsessed with the place. Following his bath, he would immediately rush to the shrine in his wet clothes to bathe the deity. Kaka was still living with his parents and siblings since his marriage. Along with other men, he would take sheep, goats and cattle to the pasture.

Kaka had total six issues. His large family included eldest Sumitra, followed by Ramkrishna, Nandubai, Murhari (me), Daivashala and the youngest Sindhu. His earnings were relatively limited to meet all the needs of the family. There was a rich family called Deshmukh near our village. They had a large expanse of farm land. Neighbouring three to four villages earned their bread and butter working in this farm. Male labourers earned one rupee and twenty-five paise per day and female labourers seventy-five paise. All these workers in fact were exploited to do hard work. All of these people were illiterate. Resultantly, despite the scanty wages, they had no other option except working there. My parents too worked there on daily wages.

Kaka had appealing personality. He was tall, muscular and had sturdy body earned by hard work. Feelings in eyes were like a tranquil sea. He wore a *tulsi-mala* and used to have *ashtagandha* on the forehead. He had such a countenance which would definitely please beholders. He always put on typical attire of a Marathwada farmer which included a pure white *pheta*, *banyan*, white *sadara* of three buttons, coarse dhoti and well built *joda* with iron bottom. He may have seemed a boorish to an urbanite but he looked appealing in this costume. Being the caretaker of goats and sheep, he did the work of a shepherd. He was very honest. Deshmukh and his assistant fully trusted him. He was employed with Deshmukh on yearly basis. He did a variety of works such as ploughing, sowing, weeding, feeding oil cake and forage to oxen, milking, etc.

Kaka never paid attention to his dress. How could he have cared for it while grazing goats and sheep, slogging as a labourer in others' farm, sweating blood and working his guts out? How could he think about his dress as he was in utter poverty? Moreover, his bent of mind was a little different. He always gave prominence to taking care of inner cleanliness than the outer. His predisposition would suggest a new aphorism – 'If water is clean, what is the need of detergent?'

> *Though sugar cane is crooked its juice is not;*
> *Why are you impressed by the outward lot?*

The above dictum of Saint Chokhoba had pervaded in Kaka's blood. In rural area houses with flooring tiles were rarely found. Earth and dust has to be there in the house smeared by cow dung and scratched by cocks and hens. Kaka's discussion used to take place in such dusty houses, on patios, in streets and wherever there was a place. While sitting he never bothered about dust and the cleanliness of his clothes. Nani had to daily wash his soiled clothes. Naturally she was annoyed of this behaviour. To vent her anger, she would babble and strike clothes against a big stone while washing them. There was nothing called applying cloth-washing bar at that time. Only washing soda was available. Hence Nani's vexation was quite natural.

For bathing, a bucket of water was sufficient to Kaka. From the same bucket he would keep back a pot of water for puja. He would himself fetch water from a well. In all seasons he would use cold water for bathing. However, he rarely had cough, cold and any other illness. I do not remember that he was ever taken to a hospital. The diseases such as asthma, blood pressure, diabetes remained far away from him.

Physically, Kaka was in worldly affairs, but by mind he was disengaged from worldly affections and passions. All the time there was a conflict in his mind. Saint Tukaram termed it as 'war.' On one hand, a person has to shoulder worldly duties and obligations, and on the other, he has unrestrained longing for spirituality. Kaka's mind was, therefore, like a fish out of water. The incidents occurred in his life were much the same. His worldly engagements and family were quite sizable. He could neither forsake them nor discontinue his divine pursuit. As a result, our mother was as sullen as Saint Tukaram's. Like the Saint, Kaka did not lose peace of mind and never let himself withdraw from his divine objective. In his *kirtans,* he not only recited *abhangas*, but he actually followed the way that was shown in them.

It was true that Kaka was a devotee but by nature he was very strict, as if another *Jamadagni*. Once Nani's mother, my grandmother had said something sarcastic about him. Since the incident, Kaka never visited the place of his in-laws. He did not tolerate impertinent remarks.

Nani: My Mother

Nani was the third daughter-in-law in Aaba Kele's family. The wives of her husband's brothers and her husband's sisters always bothered her since her marriage. Her husband never took her side because his only concern was his God. His complete absorption was divinity, not his family. When he went to Yedshi, he left his wife in Kelewadi itself. Here, the wives of her husband's brothers and her husband's sisters intensified their harassment. Besides, she was ousted from the house. She herself knew the circumstances she faced. For some more days, she tolerated this botheration. She saved some money and came to Yedshi. However, Kaka did not pay attention to her and told her to go back. Yet her mother-in-law and even mother did not support Nani. After collecting necessary things like wood, stalks of pulse tree, dry blades of sugarcane she erected her own hut. Nani and Sumitra lived in the same hut. Since Nani was working on daily wages, she had difficulty in rearing Sumitra. She was so frustrated with her life due to her troubles and the lack of support. In these circumstances, life became unbearable for Nani. The thoughts of suicide hovered over her mind. She faced a predicament here.

The Predicament

Following Kaka's instruction, Nani returned to Kelewadi from Yedshi. Her in-laws did not allow her to stay with them. As a result, she came to her mother's place. Even her mother discarded her by saying, "Since your luck is unfavourable, what can we do?" The sky fell on Nani. At that time, my eldest sister Sumitra was still a child. Like any other sensitive woman, my mother was taken aback by the situation. The thought of suicide occurred in her mind. To commit suicide, she approached a well which was half full. She was about to jump into the well but stopped awhile. She looked at the water and her little daughter flashed before her eyes. She sat by the side of the well thinking for quite a long time. She had a dilemma about what to do next. "What about Sumitra if I jump into the well. What if I first push Sumitra into the well and my plan changes afterwards? Why should I sacrifice the life of my innocent child? Never. There is much heroism in confronting adversities." With this resolution and self-assurance, she returned home.

She then valiantly conquered all the calamities. She had already left behind the place of her in-laws. Then she kept staying in her hut. The hut would leak during rainy season. Due to the leaking hut she spent most of her nights sleeplessly taking her daughter in her arms. Her means of support were daily chores such as washing of clothes and household utensils, filling of water, grinding, pounding, etc. She had to work without having eaten anything. There was nobody to support her. It is said that no one helps in difficulties. So Nani experienced this harsh reality. She had to do the donkey work the whole day in others' farm and spent her nights in the cramped hut. For Nani, her husband's presence and absence was insignificant. Nani's account of these experiences used to be hair-raising.

Kaka's Passage from Yedshi to Kelewadi

It may have happened around 1955. One day Mukta aunt's husband Bapu Kokre met Ramkrishnabhau and told him: "Bhau, your disciple Sopankaka does not look after his wife. He says that he does not want to be in domestic life. You please show the way out." Ramkrishnabhau responded, "It's alright. After returning to home, Kaka will come to the ashram. At that time, you can come to me so that I shall convince him." Kaka came to the ashram in the evening as usual. By the same time, Bapu Kokre and his wife Mukta arrived there. Then Bhau called Kaka and advised him to go back to Kelewadi with Nani. He persuaded Kaka and consequently Kaka brought Nani and resumed his wedded life. As a result, Kaka unwillingly came to Kelewadi.

Kaka's New Destination

Working as a coolie at Yedshi was very difficult for Kaka to make the ends meet. After coming back to Kelewadi, he came to know that enough wages were paid in ginning factories in north-east Maharashtra. He left Kelewadi and headed to Chikhli. Besides Kaka, so many people from our village had shifted to Buldhana and Khamgaon along with their cattle as they were displaced by famine. They lived there for a considerable period. Some of these people even today tell that Kaka used to push the 100 kg bale of cotton by his single leg.

Kaka seriously fell ill due to unfamiliar water and change in atmosphere. He stayed in Chikhli for some days and returned to Kelewadi. Physically he became very feeble. His digestive system failed and he had no control over bodily discharges like faeces and urine. He had returned in such a state. His own sisters and sisters-in-law refused to nurse and help him. Our relatives asked the question: "Why have you come to us even though you have your own healthy wife?" Since our kinsmen did not care for him, Kaka once again came to Nani. She washed his clothes, bathed him clean and started her family life afresh.

The Drought

There had been a dreadful drought in 1972. Human beings and animals could not get water to drink. Some people left the village with their cattle. So many people's livestock died during the famine. People's livelihood was ruined. Their misery knew no bounds. As Saint Tukaram says

> *Nothing to eat and nowhere to go,*
> *Staying in the village is a mere woe.*

Similar was everybody's situation. Arunojirao Deshmukh had no work to offer. Vasantrao Naik was the Chief Minister of Maharashtra during this difficult period. Under the employment guarantee scheme, he started work of road construction. I may be six or seven at that time. There had been blazing sunlight. In such heat, Kaka and Nani would draw large stones out of quarries and break them into pieces. I distinctly remember that searing summer. There hadn't been any shade to rest for sometime while breaking the road metal. All the trees had dried out. There was no water to drink. My parents indeed did the backbreaking work in that blistering heat. Sweat ran down from their body as if they were bathing. They hardly got clothes to cover their body. In their tattered clothes, they were working like *Wadars*. They were wounded by the small bits of stones they hit by their sledgehammer.

They strived arduously to quench hunger and save the lives of their four little children. They could hardly get food and clothing. I had only a half pant though I was six or seven. Occasionally, I had to remain naked. For survival, we consumed *barbada* which was not eaten even by cattle. It was intensely difficult period as this *barbada* too was sold in shops. Worm-eaten *jowar* of a strange name was available at ration shops. Half of the *jowar* was nothing but cobwebs and rubbish. We had to eat even such type of stuff. Apart from *jowar*, a little amount of wheat and wheat flour called *sukdi* was available. The names of even dogs were registered in ration cards to get this *sukdi*. The images of famine are still there in my mind. I'll not be able to forget that *barbada*, *jowar* and *sukdi* till my last breath.

There had been quite woeful condition of food. Nani would somehow borrow some flour and bake four-five *bhakris* which were not enough to all. At times, she used to rub corn ears of green *jowar* and provide it to us for eating. She would give us *bhakris* and would consume salted and pungent water drawn from boiled vegetables. My mother patiently and courageously faced adversities and surmounted the hard time.

Nani was accustomed to work in the farm during the daytime and domestic work in the home at night. As a result, she was often tired out. Getting out of bed early morning, only she had to shoulder the strenuous works such as cooking, washing kitchen utensils and clothes, bathing the children, etc. So she would get infuriated. Occasionally she used to scold us. Mostly I was the frequent target of her anger. Being a child, I had intense anger towards Nani. Afterwards her nature became quite mollifying and sensitive as she grew quite affectionate towards me.

Kaka and Nani worked very hard for all of us. We could understand the meaning of hard work when we observed our parents' drudgery. My education and sisters' marriages are the outcome of their industrious nature. They were equal to Vitthal and Rukmini for us.

CHAPTER 2

Kaka's Children

Sumitra: My Eldest Sister

Sumitra is the eldest among all of our siblings. She attended school when she was a child. She was very sharp as she would memorize the same day the lesson given by her teacher. She mastered Marathi alphabet, numbers, arithmetical tables, etc. One day her teacher complained to Kaka in sheer jest, "Kaka, what shall I teach now to your daughter? I am being pestered by this question." This was, in fact, appreciation of Sumitra's speed of learning. She attended school up to fourth standard. Her further education was discontinued as our village lacked next standards. Sumitra was quick tempered and quite inconsiderate which occasionally resulted in Kaka's beating.

At the early age of twelve, Sumitra was wedded to Shripati Bodke from Bangarwadi. I distinctly remember an incident though I fail to recall her wedding. There is a tradition in our community to offer clothes to the newly married son-in-law. So Kaka brought clothes from Washi and all the preparation was made. As instructed by his father, Sumitra's husband wanted a golden ring. He began sulking and threatened that he would not accept clothes if his demand was not fulfilled. Kaka asked him but only once, "Will you take clothes or not?" The sullen son-in-law remained tight-lipped. Kaka was infuriated. He packed the clothes and readied to return them to the shop. People present there requested Kaka to wait but to no avail. Kaka's anger was quite awful. He declared, "If he comes back he will not get clothes. Besides, Sumitra will not be sent with him." My brother-in-law was so frightened as he immediately returned to his village in despair. When he came back after some days, he could neither get new clothes nor a ring. He took Sumitra with him and left. From the incident onwards, he was always scared of Kaka. For a long time, he lacked courage to talk with Kaka.

Sumitra was very gentle and sensitive. When chided, tears would immediately appear in her eyes. On four days a week, she would have fast of certain deities. She had difficult time in her life. There is a melody in her voice. She sings songs of the Goddess Ambabai very tunefully along with proper beats. Her voice has power to enchant listeners. Her other feature is that she is quite excellent at acting. Without any flaw, she can exactly do the mimicry of any women from our village. Whenever I visited Kelewadi, we all siblings used to chat at night and cheerfully applaud her mimicry.

Sumitra has two sons namely Mukund and Bapu. The former is a senior operator in Mahatransmission (Maharashtra State Electricity Transmission Company Ltd.). The latter is a farmer. Both of them have two children. Sumitra's husband is a gentleman and his family leads happy life though their resources are limited.

Ramkrishna: My Elder Brother

Ramkrishna was the first son born to my parents. As a child, he was very plump and sturdy. He had a minor illness when he was fourteen to fifteen. Our parents had no money for his medication. His health deteriorated and he died consequently.

Kaka had made prediction about Ramkrishna. During Ramkrishna's illness, Kaka anticipated about his short life. Nani used to carry him to Washi on her shoulders. She had to borrow money from others as financial crises were very severe. Ramkrishna could not get proper treatment as required amount was not available. Many a time, Nani carried him on shoulders even when it rained but to no avail. My brother did not survive. Unfortunately Kaka's prediction proved to be right. He became victim of our parents' extreme poverty.

Nandubai: My Elder Sister

When Nanduakka was in first or second standard, I was five and obviously younger than her. I would accompany her to school which she attended up to third standard. The school lacked further standards following the third. I was admitted in first standard when Nanduakka was ten years old. Nani used to take her to the farm to take care of our younger sister Daivashala. Both Kaka and Nani were working as labourers in Deshmukh's farm. We used the title *Wahini* for the landlady. She was as good looking as Lakshmi. Her conversation was quite mellow. She was compassionate to understand the poor.

Nanduakka used to have insufficient clothes when our parents worked at the Deshmukh. She was buxom but had tattered clothes. As a result, *Wahini* would sympathise with my sister and offer used clothes. Once she had given me her son's scout uniform. Most of these clothes were in a good condition. People used to laugh at us for our condition. We were helpless though humiliated.

Deshmukh *Wahini* had deep affection for Nanduakka. Even after her marriage, *Wahini* would enquire about her. Khandekars from Wanjarwadi had come to *see* Nanduakka. Financially the family was much like us. The marriage was finalized and the dowry of five hundred rupees was agreed upon. The marriage took place. Nanduakka's husband Chandrasen Khandekar proved to be a gentleman. My sister Nanduakka is meek, tolerant and very kind. Her love towards parents was very intense. She could rarely get angry. When angry, she had the habit of grinding her teeth and chewing her lips. However, she did not beat anybody. She was quite courageous and untiring about work. She was never tired of working in her parents' home even after her marriage. She played the role of my elder brother though she was my elder sister. Her face and body are like Ahilyadevi Holkar. Her traits include loving, considerate and pacific nature. Like Sumitra, even her education was discontinued due to our poverty.

I was mostly outdoors due to my education and job. Even in my absence, she would do my work of taking our parents' care. As a result, I never felt that I have no brother to shoulder my responsibilities.

Nanduakka has two sons and a daughter. Since her husband is a nice person, she leads a good life. Her elder son Tanaji is married. He lives in Kelewadi and has a son. Sarika is

Nanduakka's daughter who lives in Chiplun after her marriage. Sarika's husband is a teacher. They have two children. Dhanaji is Nanduakka's another son who has completed the trade of Electrician from I. T. I. after his twelfth. At present, he is doing a job.

Daivashala: My Younger Sister

I was born after Nanduakka, and Daivashala was born following me. She was followed by Sindhu. As a child, Sindhu's caretaking was done by Daivashala. Daivashala even looked after a cow and a goat when she was seven or eight. She would wander in fields behind the cow. It was the time when we would at least get something to eat on time. It was because there was milk of the goat and the money we got by selling he-goats.

Daivashala was the fairest in our family. In childhood we used to chide her by calling her *Lali*. She called me *Gobrya* because I had chubby cheeks which would quiver while walking and running.

Even Daivashala could not get education. There was a specific reason behind it. Kaka and Nani were working as labourers and Sumitra was married. Nanduakka was working in Deshmukh's farm. I was getting my education and our family had no money. Daivashala had the responsibility of looking after the cow and goat. As a result, she remained illiterate.

Daivashala was betrothed to a young man called Lahu Masal. I was not present at the time of engagement since I was busy in pursuing my engineering degree. We could not afford more than fifteen hundred rupees as dowry whereas Masals wanted more. The proposed marriage was about to break.

However, the groom's side did not do that as they believed that we were good people. The groom's mother laid down a condition: "You declare that you have given us four thousand rupees as dowry. It is because another son's marriage is awaited. We will add twenty-five hundred to your fifteen hundred and I will claim to have taken four thousand as dowry." Kaka finalised the marriage and agreed upon fifteen hundred. The matter of remaining twenty five hundred was not mentioned. The wedding was done. Daivashala's brother-in-law too got married soon as her husband and his brother were twins. Both Daivashala and her sister-in-law Sindhu went to the place of their in-laws. Initially, Daivashala's mother-in-law would appreciate her for her hard work and good nature. On the other hand, the mother-in-law used to criticise Sindhu. She used to slander Sindhu and even torture her and finally tossed her out of the house. Sindhu did not have parents and she was married off by her brothers. Following Sindhu's ouster, Daivashala became lonely and her mother-in-law began harassing her. She started abusing Daivashala, Kaka and Nani and began mentioning the matter related to the dowry of twenty five hundred. When Daivashala decided to come to Kelewadi for her first delivery, her mother-in-law issued a warning: "While coming back, bring remaining twenty-five hundred rupees, else you will not enter the house."

Daivashala gave birth to a son. When it was the time of sending her back to her husband's place, she was offered clothes and ritually we bid her farewell. Now, Daivashala was doubly tortured by her mother-in-law on the issue of dowry. I assured all of them that I shall give the amount as soon as I get a job. Daivashala's in-laws were in no mood to listen. Afterwards they began teasing and beating her. Kaka was thinking to bring her back permanently as he once mentioned it. I stopped him from doing so and avoided further complications. Kaka discontinued visiting Daivashala's home.

Nani used to visit Daivashala due to her maternal love. Daivashala's mother-in-law kept abusing her and all of us including Nani and Kaka. Time changed in due course and I got a job. I gave twenty-five hundred rupees of the dowry which was not actually promised. After some years following the incident, there were some vacancies of linemen in the M. S. E. B. at Ratnagiri. After making some attempts, I got this job for Daivashala's husband. Now, their family lives in Konkan. Afterwards, their familial happiness kept increasing. Now all is well in their life. They have three children.

At present, Daivashala can read and write after getting acquainted with the alphabet by her children's help. Initially her in-laws tortured her a lot. I would plead with her in-laws though I was not that much mature. But my pleading proved to be fruitless. She has tolerated to a great extent. Being the mother of three children, now she leads quite a satisfactory family life.

Sindhu: My Youngest Sister

Sindhu was my youngest sister who was very charming. Everybody appreciated her melodious voice. She was truly obedient child. She would call me *Bhau*. When we could hardly get anything to eat every day, she used to tell Daivashala – "Let our brother eat plenty of food. His health should improve. We all four sisters have one and only brother."

Sindhu fell ill when she was seven or eight. We could not afford to take her to the private hospital. To visit the government hospital, Nani would take her on the shoulder even if there was raining. The follow-up visits were not regularly undertaken. Resultantly, Sindhu's health deteriorated. In spite of this, Kaka and Nani had to labour by leaving ailing Sindhu at home. I was busy with my schooling. Sindhu was bed-ridden as her health kept worsening. Since Kaka and Nani were at their workplace, Daivashala became Sindhu's caretaker. Her body had become quite feeble; there were no hair on her head, and her eyes had sunken. It was a desolate night during the festival of Gauri puja when Sindhu breathed her last. Much feverish Sindhu called off the journey of her life. Nani burst into uncontrolled tears which went on throughout the night. I stared and only stared at Nani's face. The following day, the dead body was covered in clothes and taken for burial. The memories of my dead sister have stuck fast in my mind even after more than four decades. Had our financial condition been good, Nani would have stayed at home to look after Sindhu. Besides Ramkisan, Sindhu became the victim of our poverty.

Me: Kaka's Son Murhari

Kaka moulded me and gave me a proper shape. I was my parents' fourth issue. After Ramkisan's death, I was my parents' only surviving son.

I was born in Kelewadi on 31st August 1966. As a child, I was very sturdy and my cheeks were quite chubby. It was the reason why people called me *Gobrya*. Because of my cheeks I looked pug-nosed. It is said that I was not a sort of cry-baby. I had the habit of playing with soil and putting it in the mouth. Consequently, I would be punished by Nani. My belly became big and hard due to the habit of eating soil. It would also have been the result of worms. All were frightened. Some rustic healers advised to cauterize on the belly and the suggestion was carried out instantly. The marks of cauterisation are still there on my belly.

Since our financial condition was bad, our parents could not gratify the basic needs of food and cloth. We all children never dogged our parents for these needs. So, it was not likely that we could get spoiled by their over-indulgence. The evil of obstinacy never touched us. We better knew that our obstinacy would be greeted with thrashing. Thus, sometimes poverty puts to death but it hones up the character at times.

It was the time when women's education was not as usual as today. Kaka enrolled the names of all the children in our school at Kelewadi despite his rural and uneducated background. Kaka shaped all of us as he had deep concern about his children. Nanduakka accompanied me when I was in first standard. All of us were quite good in our studies. Nevertheless, I was considered to be better than rest of my siblings. Once, an officer visited our school for inspection. He asked some questions to the students. We were asked to raise hand if we knew the answer. Each time I raised my hand and answered to the questions. The officer viewed me with appreciation and said "Now, I am going to ask you the last question. If you give the correct answer, I shall directly elevate you to the fourth standard." He asked me the question but I failed to recall the answer instantly. However, it struck me when I sat down and my friend answered. Anyway, I could not furnish the answer to the officer in time. Consequently, I missed the chance of getting promoted to the fourth standard. Although late, I was happy to have recalled the answer. I narrated the incident to Kaka when I reached home. He appreciated me to a great extent. It was true that he did not care for worldly life for his spiritual obsession. But it was also true that he was not indifferent towards his children.

I passed my fourth standard. It was the village Kanheri where I was enrolled in fifth standard as Kelewadi did not have next classes. Kanheri was close to Kelewadi which had grades from five to seven. I did not have proper clothes as our financial condition was still bad. I had quite funny attire which included a coarse khadi cap, a tattered and dirty shirt and a very short half pant. My pant was tattered on posteriors and resultantly was mended with multi coloured patches. Besides, I had no footwear. I rarely felt ashamed though I attended my school in strange outfits. One day a girl taunted me for my half pant through which my rear was visible. Following this I felt very embarrassed. I reported the matter to my teacher Jadhav Sir. He scolded the girl and the matter was closed. I had no grudge against the girl and the thought of revenge never entered my mind.

> *It's the god's worship and our communion,*
> *Not to envy any mortals, besides men.*

Similar to this maxim of Saint Tukaram was Kaka's disposition which I might have inherited. At that time, the examination of seventh standard was conducted by the State Board. My younger sister Daivashala was still a child when I was in seventh standard. Nanduakka was married off and was with her in-laws in Wanjarwadi. Kaka and Nani went to this village for doing work in a dam construction. As they were staying in Wanjarwadi, only I was left in Kelewadi. As a result, I was asked to stay with Nani's sister Mukta *mavshi*. Some quantity of *jowar* and other material I required was given. My school used to open at eight in the morning. In the beginning, Mukta *mavshi* would rise early to prepare meal for me. After some days, she started getting angry and I had to attend school without having eaten anything. Her conduct was quite biased as I was told to do work even on holidays. I myself had to bring cake of cow dung and fire wood. She had the least sympathy for me. Our examination centre was Washi for the board examination. Therefore, I had to go to Washi. I halted there for three days. Mukta *mavshi* neither gave me a blanket nor anything to eat. It is said that '*mavshi* should survive though mother dies.' This adage proved to be wrong in my case. I visited my teacher Jadhav Sir who offered me all sort of help. When the examination was over, I directly went to Wanjarwadi. As I could not get wholesome food while staying in Kelewadi, I suffered from nyctalopia. To remedy this illness, Nani would ask me to bring *jogwa* from five different houses and asked me to eat the offered food by seating in a corner of the hut. My mother was not an exception about superstition.

My result was declared and I got through. Kanheri did not have classes following the seventh standard. So, next option was Washi which was at the distance of five kilometres from Kelewadi. Somebody advised Kaka, "Why do you want to send your child to the school which is far away? Withdraw his name from the school." "You are right. Who gets job even after completing education? Besides, plenty of money is needed for education" – another person added. "Absolutely right! It is out of our capacity. He will be a hand in your work." The third's persuading words. But,

Judging between the fact and fiction,
He declined the majority's opinion.

Exactly like Saint Tukaram, Kaka rejected opinion of the majority and decided to educate me further. What would have happened if Kaka had bowed to the opinion of the majority?

I got admitted in Chhatrapati Shivaji School at Washi. There had been Arts and Commerce College attached to the school. Daily it was the to and fro journey of twelve kilometres on foot from Kelewadi to Washi. Still I ranked second in eighth standard and first in the ninth. At times, Kaka would visit the school to meet the head master. It means that Kaka knew the importance of education though he was miles away from it.

I decided to stay at Washi when I entered the tenth standard. Since we had no money to pay the rent, the head master allowed me and two other boys to stay in the school premises. The matter of stay was settled but what about meals? It was a difficult issue to deal with. There were two boys from our village who used to attend the school on foot as I did. They used to bring tiffin of other two boys. However, they did not bring mine. So I would start from Washi to Kelewadi. Either Kaka or Nani would start to Washi from the other side. We would meet the half way and I would come back to Washi with my tiffin. My school gave me half of the books. Remaining books and other study material I got from my friends and prepared for the examination. My school honoured me with the 'Best Student Award' and presented me the school uniform.

My examination was over. So called intelligent students were involved in misconduct during the examination. However, such a thought never entered my mind. The result was declared. I bagged the third position with 70.23 percent of marks. The students having ranked first and second had scored only three to four marks more than me. Kaka was very happy as his decision of my education proved to be fruitful. Even Nani expressed her joy. Did Nani know the difference between success and failure? She only knew that passing is good. It was quite new for her to appreciate those who have passed in examination.

I could not get proper guidance about my further education since nobody from my village had that much education. I only knew that there was eleventh standard following the tenth. I even did not know which faculty was better to chose; arts, commerce or science. Then I sought admission in eleventh science at Barshi. When I started attending lectures in the college, I used to put on my usual attire. I wore a white cap, a white shirt and a pyjama and was barefooted. The students made fun of me by calling me 'Dada Kondke.' Besides me, only one boy from our village wore the cap while attending lectures. As a result, we became the centre of attention. I felt quite awkward. Since we were from Marathi medium and the science subjects were in only English, we could not understand anything taught by the teachers. We ran away from the college and enrolled our names in eleventh commerce at Washi where we attended lectures for two weeks. After going through our mark sheets, a clerk and some teachers from the college advised us to opt for science faculty. But the science college was in Barshi. Kaka came with me and I was admitted in eleventh science in Bhausaheb Zadbuke College, Barshi. Kaka even visited Osmanabad on somebody's suggestion that technical education was even better. But it was too late to get admission there. So, my admission was finalised in the same college at Barshi. I could get accommodation in government hostel and my way to further education became quite easy. Kaka still considered me a school going boy though I was in college. During one of his visits to Barshi, he bought for me a khaki half pant. He gave me five rupees for my expenses. I had only one pyjama which I used to wear when in college. Elsewhere I had to use the half pant.

Kaka never liked us to watch films. Therefore, I did not visit theatres. Consequently, I did not have fascination of actresses. Once a program called 'Star Night' was held in our college to aid the Nargis Dutt Cancer Hospital. People had an opportunity to see many film stars in the program. Hence the program got overwhelming response. I chose to study while other boys left for the program. As a result, I scored hundred out of hundred marks in mathematics in the test conducted on the following day.

The examination of eleventh science concluded and there began summer vacation. The hostel mess was closed but I decided to continue my stay in Barshi for coaching class of the twelfth. Although my tutor did not ask for coaching fee, how could I get meals for free? Throughout the vacation, I ate only once a day.

I decided to take break during my twelfth. I had to take this decision because there was a compulsion to have the same examination board for tenth and twelfth to get admission in Engineering. I had completed my tenth from the Aurangabad Board and was about to complete twelfth from the Pune Board. So it was easy for me to take admission in engineering if I appear for the twelfth examination from Osmanabad which belonged to the Aurangabad Board. So this was my plan. Accordingly, I appeared for the examination from Osmanabad. I ranked first from all three colleges. Thus my admission to Engineering was guaranteed.

I completed B. E. Electrical from Government Engineering College, Aurangabad in 1989. In the same year I got a job in a private firm called Garware Company. At the same time, I did M. B. A. Subsequently in 1991, I was posted at Chiplun as a Junior Engineer in M. S. E. B. It was followed by my direct recruitment as an Assistant Engineer. Meanwhile I completed L. L. B. and B. J. By the same time, I was posted at Bhiwandi as a Deputy Executive Engineer through direct recruitment. After two years, I was promoted as an Executive Engineer and posted at our Mumbai head quarter 'Prakash Gad.' Then I worked at Pen and in Torrent Power Company, Bhiwandi for six months and one and half year respectively. I stood first in the state in direct recruitment for the post of Superintendent Engineer and was posted at Nagpur. In the mean time, I got through the examination called F. I. E., A. C. P. D. M. & E.A. conducted for energy auditor. Then I completed my Ph. D. in 'Power Distribution Franchise.' But I regret that Kaka is no more to appreciate me for my achievements.

I have two sons and a daughter. Ajinkya, my elder son has completed his B.Com; Vivek the younger son is in twelfth now. My loving daughter Sanskruti is in fifth standard. Manisha, my wife, is a graduate who is quite cultured and considerate. However, there is no day without the memories of Kaka.

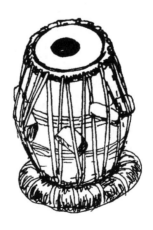

CHAPTER 3

Making the Impossible Possible through Efforts

Customarily Kaka did not get formal school education. His parents were illiterate and this trend continued in the following generation. As it was the village of shepherds, the people of Kelewadi were uneducated. How would they get education whose universe was their sheep only? I had curious respect about Kaka's scholarship. Therefore, once I asked him, "Since you were illiterate, how could you study such bulky scriptures?" Kaka replied and referred to Saint Tukaram

Attaining the unattainable is possible,
Says Tuka, through study, efforts and mettle.

He told me that the same thing he did in his life and then disclosed the mystery behind his journey from illiteracy to scholarship.

Kaka might be thirteen to fourteen. As a caretaker of sheep, he was in the service of a local landlord called Deshmukh. At that time, a Brahmin teacher used to visit the single teacher school in the neighbouring village Kanheri. Kaka too had strong impulse of getting acquainted with letters. But he was afraid of approaching the teacher. A prominent person from the village came to know about Kaka's aspiration. One day the teacher was passing from there on a horse. The villager stopped him and told the teacher, "Sopan wants to learn letters; please teach him." In this way, the man convinced the teacher who immediately consented. Then, while going to the school and coming back the teacher taught Kaka some letters. With the help of some sharp objects like a piece of earthenware and small wooden sticks, Kaka started practicing letters by writing them on the ground and even on the back of buffalos. One day the teacher did not turn up. Afterwards he never came back. It was not clear whether the teacher died or left the school. Kaka's dream of learning letters did not realise.

Yedshi: A Sacred Place

Yedshi is a village in Osmanabad district. 'Vedashree' reportedly was the old name of this village. It is believed that the nearby hills were the abode of *rishis* and *munis*. As per legends, Lord Rama was informed here itself that Ravana abducted Sita. Jatayu's residence was located in this area. He heard Sita's wailing and rushed to the place to rescue her. The following description occurs in *the Ramayana*:

After hearing Sita's wailing,
Jatayu rushed there with vexed feeling.
She is the wife of my master;
Who are you, a villain, to torture?

Jatayu halted Ravana's chariot which was followed by a deadly battle between the two. Ravana was badly wounded. He realised that he had no mettle to face Jatayu. Jatayu fell prey to Ravana's deceit and told him that his end lied in his wings. Without any delay, Ravana struck Jatayu's wings and cut them off. Ravana parted with his thumb during the clash. Jatayu became unconscious and the news reached to Rama. Rama rushed to the dying Jatayu and came to know about the battle. Moved by his chivalry, Rama granted Jatayu the *moksha*. This entire incident took place at Yedshi.

On the following day, Lord Rama worshipped Lord Shiva where Jatayu breathed last. Soon after, the place became the shrine called Ramalinga. Here itself Lord Rama performed funeral rites of Jatayu. Jatayu's *samadhi* is found at this place.

Yedshi is the seat of saints and gods. At its east is Ter, the shrine of Saint Gora Kumbhar. The famous Neelkantheshwar temple is situated at the west. At the south, Maharashtra's *Kulswamini* Tulja Bhavani resides at Tuljapur. The Paapnasheshwar temple is at the north. Approximately a century ago, here resided a holy man called Gaibinath who was from the *Nath* sect. He chose to take *samadhi*. The villagers tried to dissuade him from this undertaking but he told them, "My life has no end. You come to Kashi a year after my *samadhi*; I shall meet you there." Many elderly people claimed that the incident actually took place.

It is the place in the Balaghat hills which is consecrated by the presence of saints, sages and deities. There was a Vedashram close to the Ramalinga temple. In this Vedic school, many students regularly study *the Vedas* with great interest even today.

The place is known as the Ramalinga hill. Revered Bankatswami used to visit the hill for his studies. At this time, Ramkrishnabhau Yedshikar Maharaj and Bankatswami met. Yedshikar's *phad* flourished because of Bankatswami's blessings. Some coolies working at Yedshi railway station had joined the Yedshikar's *phad*. It was the place where sacred Gita was taught.

Kaka's elder sister Mukta's husband belonged to Yedshi. Once Mukta came to Kelewadi and spoke to Aabaji, my grandfather, "This is your pitiful condition though you have four brave sons. You send my brothers Sopan and Sambhaji to Yedshi. I shall employ them as coolies at the railway station." Accordingly she took them to Yedshi.

Bhagwanbhau and Ramkrishnabhau, the two Yedshikar brothers dwelt in Yedshi. Kaka knew some of their disciples while working as a coolie at the railway station. As a result, Kaka was attracted towards *bhajans* and *kirtans*. It was the time when Yedshikar brothers' *phad* was emerging under the guidance of Ramkrishnabhau. Throughout the day, some of the coolies used to memorise *the Bhagavad Gita*. All the day Kaka would hear notes of shlokas pronounced by his companions. Consequently, even Kaka's mind changed and he had a desire to articulate Sanskrit shlokas. Since he was illiterate, he was unable to undertake an assignment to read and memorise shlokas. His helplessness made him more uncomfortable. However, because of some good people's company he daily started visiting the ashram.

> *You turned this wrongdoer into a person fine,*
> *Into Vishnu's follower with the virtues divine.*

Therefore, companionship is of great importance. The days passed by and Kaka's restlessness kept increasing gradually.

> *Soon shall it be the state of mine,*
> *For Lord Pandurang, I shall always pine.*
> *Will He liberate me forever?*
> *Will He grant me a glance of favour?*
> *Tell me so, o saints! As you are kind,*
> *And offer ease to my anxious mind.*
> *This turmoil, this fretfulness I constantly fight,*
> *All the day and even night.*
> *It is, says Tuka beyond our strength,*
> *To get released to a proper length.*

Kaka was overwrought by the same thought. At that time, Late Rangnath Maharaj Parbhanikar used to visit Yedshi for a week. His *kirtans* and *pravachans* were daily scheduled throughout the week.

Beginning of Spiritual Life

While working as a coolie, Kaka developed interest towards *bhajans*. He became disciple of Ramkrishnabhau. Kaka used to participate in the debates which involved the topic of spirituality. One day Kaka got very important information through such a debate. He came to know that Bapu Master was that mahatma who taught *the Bhagavad Gita* to Ramkrishnabhau. Moreover, Bapu Master taught him some other scriptures. Now, Bapu Master had become very old and feeble whose eyesight had weakened. He almost lost his sight as he was very old. As a result, he could see nothing. He even did not have close relatives. Therefore, Ramkrishnabhau used to send his disciples to look after Bapu Master. Although these people were there in his service, they disliked to serve him. This made Kaka's sensible mind quite restless. He began accompanying Bhau's disciples to serve Bapu Master. Soon Kaka developed a close bond with him. He happily chose to do works like cleaning the Master's room and filling water. One day Kaka got up early morning as usual and went to Bapu Master's ashram. He smeared the ashram with cow dung. He took Bapu Master to toilet and then bathed him.

"Who is this new boy?" Bapu Master asked somebody present there. "He has newly arrived. He is the bother-in-law of a certain *Dhangar*," somebody replied. The Master nodded and said, "Alright."

Then Kaka offered his daily service to Bapu Master. His yearning to learn 'God' made him more restless. Bapu Master may have noticed Kaka's restlessness.

One day Kaka entered the Master's room. The latter was very happy. The following interaction took place between them:

> Bapu Master: What work do you do?
> Kaka: I am a coolie at the railway station.
> Bapu Master: Do you attend *bhajans*?
> Kaka: Yes, I do; but know nothing about them.
> Bapu Master: So, what is your plan?
> Kaka: I want to learn 'God'.
> Bapu Master: (*Laughing*) What do you want to learn?
> Kaka: 'The Bhaagwat Gita.' (Once again the Master laughed).

> Bapu Master understood that he wanted to learn 'the
>   Bhagavad Gita.'
> Bapu Master: (Raising his finger) I see! From that shelf,
>   take out the third book tied in cloth.
> Kaka said 'Yes' and immediately brought the book.
> Bapu Master: Now open a certain page and read it.
> Kaka: How can I? I am illiterate.
> Bapu Master: Then how will you learn?
> Kaka: As the teacher you recite first. Then I will
>   follow you.

Bapu Master smiled and slowly pronounced each word
and Kaka imitated him. Then the Master would recite a shloka
every day in front of Kaka followed by Kaka's recitation. So
Kaka used to memorise the shloka all the day and come back
to the ashram at night.

> Bapu Master: So, do you recall what we learned in the
>   morning?
> Kaka: Yes.
> Bapu Master: Then recite it.

Then Kaka would clearly recite the shloka. Bapu Master
would respond to him by nodding his head. The Master began
teaching the fifteenth chapter of *the Bhagavad Gita*. Kaka
exactly imitated the Master's recitation though he understood
nothing. He memorised the entire chapter with the routine
of two shlokas a day. The Master was elated. Subsequently
Kaka was asked to memorise the twelfth chapter followed
by ninth. Afterwards Kaka began from the first chapter and
memorised the complete *Bhagavad Gita* along with *the Vishnu*

Sahasranama. Following this, he learned reading and writing. Having achieved this success, he never looked back in terms of scholarship.

The complete *Bhagavad Gita, the Vishnu Sahasranama,* etc. were at the tip of Kaka's tongue. His spiritual splendour gradually soared. Kaka's such hardship was very exceptional as once he was an illiterate layperson. He attained the unattainable.

Once, Ramkrishnabhau recited a shloka during his *pravachan.* He asked his disciples about the serial number of the shloka and the chapter in which it appears. None of them responded. However, Kaka provided the right answer. Bhau was so happy and he asked, "From whom have you taken your lesson?" Kaka replied, "From guru Bapu Master." Bhau patted Kaka on the back and appointed him as the *chopdar* in his *phad.* Through intense hard work and great efforts, Kaka made his spiritual life very fruitful. Kaka's basic disposition was detachment as he was not interested in familial life. It was therefore he initially opposed to marry. Later, he changed his mind and got married only to respect elders.

Kaka's craving was similar to Saint Tukaram's. Kaka's reading included *the Shaddarshane, the Four Vedas, the Eighteen Puranas, the Brahma-sutra-bhashya, the Dnyaneshwari, the Navnath, the Harivijay, the Adwait Amogh, the Vichar Sagar-Rahasya, the Tukaram, the Namdev, gathas* of all saints and many rare scriptures. He not only read them but also reflected and meditated after his reading. He even adhered to their teachings in his day-to-day life.

Such erudition of an illiterate person is quite spectacular. Kaka achieved the unachievable through his study. In due course, his thinking and behaviour changed. He memorised many *abhangas* from Tukaram *Gatha*. He became an excellent *kirtankar* while delivering *pravachans*. With this he crossed the first step of spiritual life.

Kaka's Encounter with a Holy Man

Kaka narrated how once he had a confrontation with a holy man. Kaka told: "On every Sunday we had holiday. As a result, we would plan to visit the Ramalinga hill on every Sunday. Since it was the holy month of Shravan, many pilgrims were seen around. Above the streams, there were two rooms on the ridge. I went there to wash my clothes. A holy man was already there, drying his clothes after bathing. I washed my clothes and laid them out to dry. Meanwhile the holy man had entered the nearby room. I had to wait there to collect my clothes after they dry. Then why not chat with the man for now? So I moved close to the room. The holy man had closed the door and seated for *pranayama*. He had drawn his tongue out of the mouth. It was clear that he was busy in yoga. Nevertheless, I knocked the door. Instantly the holy man roared like a tiger and the hills reverberated because of the sound. I ran towards the temple, leaving my clothes behind. I was very frightened. What to do now? I had put on only dhoti. Rest of the clothes were left behind, drying near the room. By that time, I met my brother-in-law Bapu Kokre. He had come there for *darshan*. I was so happy to find him there. I said, 'I left my clothes near the pond.'

He asked, 'But why?'

'I cannot go back there alone,' I said.

'But why? Where did you wash your clothes?'

I replied, 'I was not scared while washing clothes on the ridge. But I heard a tiger's roaring from the room and ran away in the present condition. Now, I will not go alone to bring my clothes.'

Then both of us headed towards the place and brought my clothes."

Kaka termed the incident a miracle. For him Ramalinga became the place of devotion. Even Saint Dnyaneshwar urged for the *Pasaydan*. He expected: "May all the living beings get whatever good is there in this world; may they come in contact with godly people." Kaka believed that he had an encounter with such an ascetic.

Late Bankatswami's Attachment to Yedshi

Ramkrishnabhau was a leading cloth merchant from Yedshi. His conduct was quite virtuous. For his studies, saintly Bankatswami used to visit and reside at Ramalinga hill, at Kapildhara in Beed district and even at Bhandara hill near Dehu. As these places were very serene, Bankatswami would stay there for months. Lots of people would assemble for Bankatswami's *Kakda bhajans*. Nowadays such a gathering is rarely found for *kirtans* of even leading *kirtankars*. Bankatswami's singing was very harmonious and his memorising quite impressive. During his stay at Ramalinga, the Yedshikar brothers would look after his food.

One day Bankatswami's meal could not reach in time. Ramkrishnabhau's younger brother Bhagwanbhau was late to deliver meal to Bankatswami. Bhagwanbhau was very frightened while returning from the Ramalinga hill as the night approached. It was a distant place from Yedshi. The jungle had deep valleys and it was under the control of Forest Department. So, tigers, hyenas, wolves, snakes and all sorts of animals freely loitered there. Bhagwanbhau could not stay with Bankatswami as it was the latter's observance of silence. Thus, Bhagwanbhau was so confused. By that time, Swamiji came out of the cave and took his meal. He would consume fruits and milk only. Following this he would take the veena in his hand and begin his nightlong *bhajans.* Today, many people are needed for a *bhajan.* Besides, a good *mridanga* player is a must. It is seen nowadays that the tabla has replaced the *mridanga* and the harmonium has taken the place of veena. Saint Tukaram says,

> *We shall fondly relish divine pleasure;*
> *The melody of mridanga, cymbals, veena*
> *and his name is our treasure.*

By taking veena in his hand, Bankatswami was busy in his *bhajans* near the river Pitali. Following *Kakda Aarti,* he concluded his *bhajans* in the dawn. Until now Bhagwanbhau was sitting close to the river. He did not sleep a wink.

> *Who cares this mortal measure?*
> *When blessed with divine pleasure.*

Similar was Bhagwanbhau's feeling which Swamiji noticed. Setting aside his observance of silence, he called Bhagwanbhau to him and said, "Bhagwan, send Ramkrishnabhau to me. I want to talk to him." Bhagwanbhau departed and delivered the message to Ramkrishnabhau. The latter went to Bankatswami and asked him, "What is the matter?"

> *You are, says Tuka, so benevolent and mellow at heart,*
> *To admire this child and to make him smart.*

Then Swamiji took Bhagwanbhau to Pandharpur and bought a *pakhawaj* at his own cost. He trained Bhagwanbhau in such a way and made him proficient in playing *pakhawaj.* However, he sent Bhagwanbhau to Varanasi for further education. Throughout his life, Swamiji remained celibate. Swamiji's disciple Bhagwanbhau followed his guru's example and became an exemplary player of *pakhawaj.* Yedshikar's *phad* was the outcome of his efforts. At this *phad,* five hundred *taalkaris* would participate in a *kirtan.* This *phad* had its influence across Maharashtra.

Bankatswami's Meeting with Mandaleshwar

Once, a group of pilgrims from Varanasi visited Alandi. It was the time when Bankatswami's *Harinam Saptah* was held there. Mandaleshwar from Varanasi was so impressed by the program. He said, "There are so many holy places and even big temples in Utter Pradesh. But nowhere is the pleasure of *bhajans* that is found in Maharashtra. Therefore, Maharashtra is superior."

Swamiji requested Mandaleshwar, "Maharaj you deliver a *kirtan.*" Mandaleshwar instantly replied, "I am really sorry as I cannot do this since I lack the knowledge of *Prakrit.* You may ask me to deliver a *pravachan* in Sanskrit the whole day, but I fail to deliver a *kirtan* in Marathi."

Swamiji said, "Please, you just stand up and begin your *pravachan.* We shall handle rest of the matter." Mandaleshwar delivered *kirtan* for two hours. He was completely absorbed in the *kirtan* as Swamiji contributed the required *abhangas* with tuneful singing. Swamiji would simplify Mandaleshwar's Sanskrit interpretation in Marathi. As a result, Mandaleshwar was so delighted. Finally he said, "Although I am called as a pedant in Sanskrit, you are undoubtedly a master in Marathi." So this Swamiji used to stay at Ramalinga Shrine for four months. Like Saint Tukaram, he too loved solitude.

Kaka's first *Kirtan*

Chaturmas was very important period of learning for Kaka. During this period he used to listen to *pravachans* of many imminent scholars, including Rangnath Maharaj Parbhanikar. During this period of four months, these scholars used to stay in Pandharpur. Rangnath Maharaj was an authority in Tukaram as so many pedants like Dhunda Maharaj Deglurkar, Appasaheb Waskar, Manohardada Gosavi would attend his *kirtans*. After listening to all these prominent people, Kaka became so proficient in explicating any difficult topic.

Since Ramkrishnabhau had fathomed Kaka's scholarship, once he asked Kaka to deliver a *kirtan* in a *Saptah*. Kaka declined the offer very politely. He said, "Bhau, I am not able to do it. I am an illiterate person. I shall not deliver *kirtan* as it's your grand event." Bhau's *Saptah* would involve eight *pakhawaje* and two to four-hundred *taalkaris*. It was a difficult task to deliver *kirtan* in such a congregation. Bhau warned Kaka in clear words, "If you do not deliver a *kirtan*, then there will not be any *kirtan* at all." A huge audience used to come there in bullock-carts from the nearby villages for the program. Kaka was alarmed to see the large gathering. He declared, "I am not able to deliver *kirtan* as I lack that much courage." Bhau insisted as, "Kaka, you must do it." Then Kaka summoned courage and stood up for *kirtan*. He would tell us that he was shivering with fear. Till then he never spoke before public. "Now, it was the time to stand before no other but Ramkrishnabhau and deliver *kirtan*. However, Bhau encouraged me and I rose with boldness. Saint Dnyaneshwar's *abhanga* was chosen for the *kirtan*."

> *When the guru is to support and always bless,*
> *Why others' help and their needless mess.*
> *Will king's wife ever beg? No, never,*
> *Only mind rules her always, however.*
> *As the person sitting below a wish fulfilling tree,*
> *Gets anything whatever it may be.*
> *Likewise, Dnyandev says, I am liberated forever,*
> *With my guru's blessings and his favour.*

Kaka's selection of the *abhanga* was very suggestive as seen above. Through the *abhanga*, he expressed his devotion towards his guru, his self-confidence and even politeness. Kaka told, "I did not notice how those two hours passed though it was my first *kirtan*. Throughout the *kirtan*, Bhau encouraged me with his smile which added to my enthusiasm. When the *kirtan* ended, Bhau pointed out my shortcomings. Finally, he patted on my back with appreciation."

This incident onwards, Kaka became a *kirtankar* and initiated the journey of his *kirtans* and *pravachans*. He began feeling uncomfortable in his domestic life. Then he studied various sacred writings such as *the Vrittti Prabhakar, the Vivek Sindhu, the Chatushloki Bhagwat* and reflected over them.

Subsequently, he delivered thousands of *kirtans, pravachans* and organized many *Harinam Saptahas* till the end of his life. He made people to do *Parayanas* of various scriptures and led them to the path of spirituality and devotion.

He aimed at social awakening by remaining active in *Warkari* sect. He delivered *kirtans* at so many places, but never accepted money for the purpose, because he believed

> ***Let's not have food at the place,***
> ***Where kirtan is delivered for His grace.***

On the other hand, he used his money for *bhajans* and social work. In this way, Kaka traversed from illiteracy to literacy, from literacy to *Prakrit*, from *Prakrit* to Sanskrit, from Sanskrit to exemplary spirituality. Finally, he attained *mukti* via *bhakti* with the help of unrivalled scholarship.

CHAPTER 4

Transformation of Kelewadi with the help of Cymbal and *Mridanga*

Dawning of change in Kelewadi

Kaka stayed at Yedshi around eighteen to twenty years. It might be the period roughly from 1940 to 1958. It was the holy place of Ramalinga Shrine where he came in a close contact with Ramkrishnabhau, Bhagwanbhau and Bapu Master who transformed him completely. Kaka returned to Kelewadi after his twenty-year association with Ramkrishnabhau. These twenty years endowed Kaka with long lasting spiritual experience. People of Kelewadi were eagerly waiting for him. He disliked customs of his village and its ways of upbringing. Most people had goats and sheep. As a result, all of them used to eat meat. Even Kaka's parents and siblings were not an exception. Therefore, Kaka was much bothered by this meat eating.

He considered his village a graveyard which lacked the music of cymbals and *mridanga*. For Kaka, the place devoid of *kirtan* and *pravachan* was equal to a graveyard. It was Kaka who instituted the practice of *bhajans* when he returned from Yedshi. Hitherto dozens of goats were killed. People would devour that type of mutton whose gravy was intensely pungent. They were untouched by education and even *bhajan*. So, it was an extremely difficult task to develop interest towards *bhajan* among these people.

Kelewadi lacked necessary culture to begin *bhajans*. From religious point of view, it lacked favourable atmosphere since most people belonged to *Dhangar* community in which nomadic songs were sung. Nobody was ready to follow the line of *bhajan* as it required pattern of sounds, rhythm, etc. The nomadic songs did not require all such things. As a result, they would turn to songs of goddesses and related pattern of words. So, Kaka found it difficult to settle in Kelewadi. His mind was in turmoil.

Meanwhile, an incident added to Kaka's frustration. Behind Kaka's residence, there was a wedding ceremony in a large house. As per the custom, nine goats were sacrificed. The smell of meat-cooking reached Kaka when he was reading *Dnyaneshwari* by sitting in front of his house. Immediately he left the place and came to Lower Kelewadi. He summoned some people there and told them that he would stay in the village only if somebody offers him a piece of land for his new settlement. Else, he would leave the village. All the people gathered there and unanimously requested him to stay as they would make arrangements of the land. Kaka's relative namely Babu Bhise requested Kaka to stay in his house.

On the following day, Kaka left Upper Kelewadi and settled in the Lower. Subsequently people brought tin sheets and erected an ashram for Kaka where he gradually began *bhajans.*

Some documents including Kaka's handwritten papers and records in Bhoom Tehsil office underline the date when Kaka began *bhajan* in Kelewadi. With the blessings of Ramkrishnabhau and Bhagwanbhau, he commenced *bhajan* on 17 July 1958.

For the purpose of *bhajan,* Kaka bought bronze-brass cymbals from Ahmednagar. From Pandharpur, he brought a *mridanga*, veena and harmonium. So a *mridanga* and thirteen cymbals were made available. It was Kaka who, for the first time, began the music of cymbal and *mridanga* in Kelewadi. Initially he himself would play the *mridanga*. Later he taught it to Saudanana Chothave who became the first person playing *mridanga*. Then he taught it to some sharp boys from the village who also became proficient players. Some of them learned playing harmonium. Kaka would look very impressive when he put veena around his neck. The notes of *bhajans* that Kaka sang buzz in my ears even today. Still I am taken aloft by the upsurge of those rapturous notes. Kaka laid the foundation of *bhajans* in our village and this practice is daily continued even now. He shaped the lives of so many disciples but never harboured its exhibition. His main preoccupation was Lord Vitthal. Therefore, he would never mention difficulties in earthly life. His main obsession and intrinsic yearning was spreading *bhajan* culture, cultivating divine adherence and imbibing virtuous upbringing among people. He firmly believed that addiction and disputes lead villages astray whereas *bhajans* and *kirtans* make their prospects promising.

Kaka decided to stay in Babu Bhise's house. With this began his daily *bhajans*. He formed a group of workers from the village which started its work of digging wells nearby Washi. Then Kaka did *parayan* of *the Harivijay Kathasar* in Babu Bhise's house. He chose Bhise's cattle shade to begin his *bhajan*.

Kaka himself would play the *mridanga* and sing *bhajans*. People started getting attracted towards his sweet-sounding *bhajans*. The villagers began participating in *bhajans* day by day. These people included Baburao Bhise, Dagdu Chothave, Saudanana Chothave, Bhau Bhalekar, Rangnath Bhalekar, Namdev Chothave, Manik Kamble and some others. Even some women like Begda Kakoo, Savitri Kakoo also joined. Kaka felt at home in the village as many responsible people supported his spiritual cause. Dagduanna Chothave built a small ashram for Kaka which is turned into Vitthal temple now.

Kaka asked his companions to learn *abhangas* by heart. He taught letters to those who were illiterate. Subsequently, these people memorised *abhangas*. Whenever there were the programs of *bhajan* in the neighbourhood of Washi, Kaka would never miss the chance. Bajirao Chothave would get the chance of the opening *chal* in Kaka's *kirtans*. Kaka's honeyed oration would make his *kirtans* very engaging.

> ***Though they don't wear basil beads' wreath,***
> ***Such chaste minds are fine with words sweet.***

However, Kaka wore a *tulsi-mala*. He transformed people from meat eaters who used to admire nomadic songs of deities to the members of *Warkari* culture. He put on *tulsi-mala* around the neck of elderly people. These senior people would bring youngsters to *bhajans*. As a result, youngsters developed interest in *bhajans*. The Gadhave family was vegetarian from the beginning. Tukaram Gadhave of the family became a special *Warkari* and Kaka's important assistant. Baburao Gadhave was the temple-priest at the Ballav Rishi Shrine who also joined *bhajans*. Gana Aaba too joined. Kaka scheduled these *bhajans* twice a day. In morning, it was *Kakda Aarti bhajan* and regular *bhajan* in the evening. On the occasion of Krishna Janmashtami, a *Saptah* was held. But some old fashioned illiterate people claimed that meat eating itself is as per their religion and they opposed the program. These people would always hinder many devotional activities such as *bhajan* and other related events.

It was a tough time for farmers as there were no rains following the sowing. As a result, they were extremely worried. Some orthodox people began criticising Kaka. They declared that approaching drought was the outcome of Kaka's *bhajan*. It underscores superstitious attitude of ignorant villagers.

Whenever Ramkrishnabhau organised *Saptahas* at Yedshi as well as at Pandharpur, Kaka would deliberately join them along with his *bhajan* companions expecting that Bhau would keep an eye on him and his people.

Kaka was determined to mould his village. The elderly people were so adamant to change. They would disdain even constructive thoughts by saying that the kid tried to teach them wisdom. It was therefore Kaka decided to shape youngsters in terms of spiritual advancement.

Kaka's Fondness for *Bhajan*

Kaka's unfailing daily routine involved his regular *bhajans*. He would get invitations of *kirtans* from the nearby villages. He always bubbled with enthusiasm during his *bhajans* and *kirtans* in evening though he had to do intense hard work of digging wells or pits. He would ask his companions to get ready to accompany him for *kirtan*. Then by taking a lantern or a torch, all of them would leave, making their way through hills and vales. Sometimes they would travel by a bullock-cart. Kaka would spend there the whole night for *kirtan*, *jagar* and *Kakda Aarti* in early morning. He would come back to home for bathing in morning. So he was habituated to this hardship. He never missed any invitation of *kirtans*. He would, in fact, never get even a single penny through *kirtans* and *bhajans*. Despite his sleepless nights, he used to do the backbreaking hard work of a labourer in the farm. Nevertheless, laziness and boredom were miles away from him. Moreover, illness never touched him.

> *Absolutely costless is His name,*
> *Of Pandurang and His acclaim.*
> *His name is nectar with essence fine;*
> *Who dwells in everybody's heart, besides mine.*

Kaka's concern was quite similar to the above maxim of Saint Narhari Sonar.

Once Ramkrishnabhau told Kaka, "Your *bhajans* are quite satisfactory but there seems to be a difficulty concerning the players of *mridanga*. For a couple of years, you send a boy to us so that we will teach him *mridanga* and make him perfect." No parents would prefer to send their son to a new place for two years. One day Kaka raised this issue to his companions when the *bhajan* was over. Neelaakka and Dagduanna stated, "Kaka, we're ready to send our son Sadashiv." At that time, Sada Tatya was only eleven to twelve. However, he was sent to Yedshi where he learnt playing *mridanga* for two years. Additionally he achieved the title *'Mridanga Mani'* in five years. Even Waskar Maharaj was amazed by Tatya's skill. Afterwards, even Bapu Chothave became an excellent player of *mridanga*.

Beginning of *Bhajans* in Upper Kelewadi

Now there was no scope for shortcoming regarding *bhajans*. People from nearby villages viewed Kelewadi with respect. Consequently, even Upper Kelewadi started following the example of the Lower. Many people chose to wear *tulsimala*. The practice of animal sacrifice at the time of marriage was permanently stopped. It was followed by unity between Upper and Lower Kelewadi. Both the villages started organising *kirtans* and *Saptahas* unitedly. Then a *dindi* from our village started visiting Pandharpur. Our village produced so many *taalkaris* and *pakhawajwadaks*. The reputation of our village spread not only across Bhoom taluka but it also reached Osmanabad, Latur, Solapur and Pune.

Kaka's Alandi to Pandharpur *Wari* on Foot

Once Kaka narrated his experiences related to *Wari*: "Our group of ten to twelve people went to Alandi for *Ashadhi Wari*. We joined Bhayyaji Maharaj Jalgaonkar's *dindi* and walked on foot from Alandi to Pandharpur. The following year, our group of twenty five people once again went to Alandi to join the *dindi*. However, we were not accommodated in the

Jalgaonkar *dindi*. At that time, Balu Thobde from Washi told us to join the *dindi* of Manohardada Gosavi Pandharpurkar. Manohardada accommodated all of us. Since then we are with the same *dindi* nearly for forty years. I am not able to walk in *dindi* since last ten years because of my age." Afterwards, Kaka used to send his disciples in the same *dindi* and would insist them, "Never leave Manohardada's *dindi*." Throughout his life, Kaka never missed even a single *Wari* to Pandharpur and Alandi.

Kaka would utter God's name even while working. He delivered *kirtans* at so many places including Balnath Chincholi, Latur, Ter, Sarola, Paithan, Dehu, and Trimbakeshwar. In spite of his failing health, Kaka remained present in the *Saptah* organized by Manohardada at Trimbakeshwar. Kaka was present there on all seven days though his health was not doing well.

Once, Kaka had been on a pilgrimage with Kisan Maharaj Sakhare. It was a month-long journey from Dattatreya's seat Mount Girnar to Alandi. Kaka climbed the mountain at the age of seventy-eight. His companions witnessed Kaka's unfailing spirit.

Kaka's only absorption was *bhajan* though he went on pilgrimages to various holy places. The pleasant clamour of cymbals and *mridanga* was his consistent attachment. He believed that this sound transported him closer to the almighty. He used to tell that, like Saint Tukaram, God always accompanied him as his comrade. Kaka and Nani always did intense hard work. At times they had to walk for ten kilometres to reach the place of work. It would take two hours to reach there. Kaka never spent this time of journey in a mere chit-chat. He would take out a book from his bag and read it while walking. The word '*Wari*' means errand or trip. It is a journey to and fro. Thus Kaka's journey to his workplace was a kind of *Wari* for him through which he worshiped his other god called work. This kind of *Wari* gradually made him attain spiritual enlightenment. Never ever he missed his *Ashadhi* and *Kartiki Wari* to Pandharpur, Alandi and Dehu. He visited these places every year as a rule to meet his beloved God Vitthal.

For so many years, Kaka did this *Wari* very regularly. As per my information he did the *Wari* for more than fifty years. When the time of *Wari* approached near, he would forget all sorts of his works and even familial responsibilities. Lord Vitthal, his only destination would beckon him. After joining the *dindi* to Pandharpur, his state of mind would reach its euphoric state. While on *Wari*, he used to carry what *Warkaris* call it '*hadpi*' all the time. It was a sack with two compartments; one for clothes such as blanket, carpet, apparel and the other was reserved for eatables. Like his innumerable compatriots, Kaka always preferred to happily eat whatever foodstuff he carried. Every time he was rapt as he was immersed in *bhajan, kirtan, bharud, gaulani.* While enunciating Dnyanoba-Tukaram, encamping and journeying ahead day by day, Kaka would march along with palanquins of Dnyaneshwar Mauli and Tukaram Maharaj. Throughout his life, Kaka devotedly did his *Wari*.

You are benign and your life, speech, even mind;
You, the Warkari of Rukmini's soul mate, are very kind.

Kaka had more dedication to his God Lord Vitthal than his day-to-day hard work. He could hardly notice when he attained sainthood and divinity. How could we notice it? About him it can be stated –

> **When I went to behold my God, my dear;**
> **I myself became God, you can see clear.**

We realised that Kaka had excelled to godliness. But it was only after his departure from this mundane world to the abode of perpetual peace.

> **Wherever I go, you are my companion, a friend true,**
> **Making me walk and guiding me through.**

Kaka: An Ever-glowing Flame

Kaka's daily routine was like an ever glowing flame in a temple. As soon as the cold water touched his body at the time of bathing, he would instantly begin chanting of particular shlokas from *the Gita Stuti*.

Beginning with these shlokas from *the Bhagavad Gita*, he would then begin chanting its fifteenth chapter. It would be followed by *Pandurangashtak* and some more shlokas. His ritualistic bathing would continue for fifteen minutes. Then his puja used to begin with putting *ashtagandha* on the image of Lord Vitthal. Next to this, he would draw with finger two lines of *gopichandan* beginning from his nose to tuft. He would put a tika of *gopichandan* and *ashtagandha* at the centre of his forehead. Then the basil plant would get water of his puja.

Kaka would get hungry by this time. Nani was habituated to rising early to do her morning chores including sweeping and smearing the hearth. She would begin cooking between seven and eight. Before this, Kaka would need breakfast. For breakfast, he would do with the previous night's *jowar bhakri* and *bhaji* or milk. Occasionally, he would never mind to have edible oil and chutney.

> **Vaishnavas' belief is the omnipresence of their God;**
> **All differences are base and void as same is the Lord.**

Following this line of thought, all sorts of prejudices were far away from Kaka. By 8 O'clock in the morning, people would throng our house to seek Kaka's advice on various issues. Besides Kelewadi, people from other villages would meet Kaka. They wanted Kaka's guidance on varied matters such as difficulty in arranging marriages, to finalise the auspicious day of the wedding which was already fixed. Somebody wanted Kaka's advice to construct a house or dig a well. People with missing articles also sought Kaka's aid. It would take two hours to address people's issues. So, Kaka would deal with such affairs between 8 and 10 in the morning.

After this, Kaka and Nani would leave to reach the workplace. Their work included slogging at the side of dams constructed by the government, digging of wells for farmers and pits of the Forest Department. Nani had to cook in the evening regardless of her exhausted condition resulting from the backbreaking work.

> **It's life, yes life, you see my dear,**
> **With plenty of pains and much fear.**
> **You get your fruits and even bread,**
> **When drops of sweat and tears are shed.**

Alike these lines by Bahinabai, Nani had to actually undergo adversities in her life.

Kaka faced financial difficulties for so many years in his life. He had to maintain balance between his worldly liabilities and spiritual life. Kaka's nephew Dattuappa reported an incident. In 1987, Kaka had sent him a letter in which he wrote, "Datta, I have planned to visit Alandi. For this purpose, I have borrowed some money. When I will come there, give me some money so that I can go to Pandharpur." Even Dattuappa's financial condition was not good. However, he resolved to bear every year the expenses of Kaka's pilgrimage from Alandi to Pandharpur. Kaka would visit Dattuappa during his *Wari*. Dattuappa would look after Kaka's expenses of *Wari* whenever Kaka went to him. Kaka stopped seeking Dattuappa's help when I got a good job.

CHAPTER 5

We Better Understand *the Vedas*

Kaka had strong passion for reading. Following his puja, he would read at least for half an hour. A bag would always hang down his shoulder in which he used to carry a book and tobacco pouch.

Sometimes, Kaka used to visit Washi for certain work on the day of weekly bazaar or even on some odd days. He had the habit of resting under a tree on the way. He used to read even while resting and disliked to waste even a single minute. All the time he was possessed by reading only. People would never find Kaka without his books. On occasions, he had to visit some places besides Washi. So, he would utilise the time of his journey on foot by reading. Sometimes he would hit his toes against stones which would result in bleeding. Kaka hardly cared his wounded toes. He would rarely pay attention to people's salutation because of his engrossment in the book. Such was his obsession with reading.

In brimming illumination of autumn moon,
Moon bird feasts on tender beams soon.

The autumn is mellow; however, the autumn moon is mellower. The young moon birds savour the moon beams amiably. In the same way, Kaka would relish books. He had read so many books again and again. Once I could not stop asking him, "Why do you read the same books repeatedly?" He instantly replied, "After every reading of the same book, I discover its newer meanings. Therefore, I choose to read it over and over." This type of reading by Kaka is termed as 'reading between the lines.' It is the real motive behind every reading which Kaka was aware of.

Illustrations of an array of *abhangas*, poetic lines, and shlokas would crowd on Kaka's lips during his *kirtan* or *pravachan*. His newest renderings would easily enthrall the audience.

Throughout his life, Kaka nurtured reading. So many excellent books were available in his collection. He would take every care to properly bind the books. He cared for his books as if a child. He took every care to maintain their sanctity. He was deadly against the defilement of the books arising from the contact of profane objects.

Kaka disregarded all sorts of bodily pleasures. He would use cold water for bathing throughout all the seasons. He did not use soaps while bathing. Of course, his financial condition was not good. When asked about this, he would say, "This body is mortal. Then why decorate it?" He would rather prefer inner purity. He used to underscore his stand by quoting Tukaram:

> *This mortal body will one day go;*
> *The cruel time eats it slow.*
> *When mind is impure, filled with vice,*
> *This learning is useless and nothing nice.*

Kaka: A Divine Personage

Kaka attained the unattainable only because of his extensive reading. He had achieved mystical and supernatural powers. Some incidents underline that he had some divine power. His usual statements would prove to be true. It was also true that his statements had a scientific base. He could read and interpret the almanac. He could associate the references from *the Sahadev Bhadli* with the almanac and forward his opinion. He had so many books in his collection. They included the *Daate Panchang* which comprised details such as the Zodiac Signs, *Nakshtra, Naadi, Gan,* etc. Kaka had a sound knowledge of all these things. The kinsmen of newborn children would come to Kaka to know the child's zodiac sign and its prospects. He would advise them about certain rituals for the removal or prevention of calamities, troubles and the like.

While arranging marriages, some people would come to Kaka to seek his advice. It included how many attributes of the boy and girl could match; would the marriage last or not and so on. He would suggest the auspicious time to begin construction of a house, to purchase farm land, to dig a well, etc. People would ask him some other questions including whether a person's bore well would be successful or not; in which *Nakshtra* it would rain; the vehicle of *Sankranti* and its impact on the year; the happenings at the national level and so on. Kaka had to answer all these questions.

Those people, having lost their articles and lives-stocks would visit Kaka for his advice. The following conversation took place between Kaka and a man whose cow was lost:

Conversation 1

Man: Kaka, my cow is lost.

Kaka: When?

Man: Since yesterday it hasn't turned up. Shall I find it?

Kaka: Yes, you will.

Man: But when and where?

Kaka: Head northward for two miles. You will find your cow grazing in a farm at your left side.

In a couple of hours the farmer would come back merrily to tell that he spotted his cow.

Conversation 2

"I lost my ring. Has somebody stolen it?"

"A mouse! Your ring is there in a hole near the hearth."

The person would come back with the news as he could locate the ring as directed by Kaka. Such type of incidents often occurred. There were some questions which would test Kaka's abilities.

Many of Kaka's predictions proved to be true. Even people had realization about them, and as result, their faith in him affirmed. People from nearby villages would come to him with some problems but return with contentment. However, it was not the case that he would speak in their favour to make them happy. Kaka would articulate only truth which stemmed from some scientific base. Moreover, he would also keep in mind the well being of society.

Once a man visited Kaka. The following conversation occurred between the two:

> Kaka: Yes Tukaram, why are you here?
>
> Tukaram: Kaka somebody stole my rooster.
>
> Kaka: Who stole it?
>
> Tukaram: I would not have come to you if I already knew it. Who stole it Kaka?
>
> Kaka: I shall not disclose the name. The person stealing it has already eaten it after cutting and roasting. Then quarrelling now is useless. I said, I am not going to tell the person's name.
>
> Tukaram: At least tell me how he looks like.
>
> Kaka: I never tell it to anybody. I don't want my people to fight among themselves. You may go now.

It was the dwelling of simple, poor and illiterate people. Accordingly were their problems which had full potential to profoundly influence their lives. As noted earlier, Kaka's prophesy mostly proved to be true. An example can be cited in this connection.

Bapu Chothave was Kaka's companion in his *bhajans* whose son died in a motor-cycle accident. Kaka had made a prophecy about the boy when he was born. Kaka had warned that the boy should be cautious of road accident at the age of twenty-two. In spite of this apprehension, the boy's destiny dragged him to death.

On the day of Makar Sankranti, Kaka would sit in Maruti temple and tell his impressions with the help of *Panchang* and *Sahadev Bhadli*. These details included rain, drought, political affairs, etc. during the upcoming year. So many people used to gather there to listen to Kaka as most of his speculations in past proved to be accurate. On this day, his forehead would become completely red due to *kumkum*. Everybody would offer him *teel-gul* and bow before him. All viewed Kaka as a virtuous and divine personage.

Kaka read a variety of scriptures, interpreted them and then meditated on them. He assimilated teachings from those books and actually behaved in accordance with their tenets.

> *That person is worthy of veneration,*
> *With no gap between speech and action.*

Kaka was therefore revered by people. He found his Lord Vitthal far and wide and his life was surmounted by Him. Kaka had overcome all sorts of vices and led an illuminating kind of life. Through his self-experience, he even brightened the lives of so many people.

Kaka: A Speculative Scholar

Customarily, Kaka could not get formal education. His learning gradually progressed through his journey from illiteracy to literacy and from unflinching efforts. His scholarship kept on moving upward because of his gurus Ramkrishnabhau and Bapu Master. In his early life, he took lessons and memorised all eighteen chapters of *the Bhagavad Gita* including *the Vishnu*

Sahasranama. His fondness of spirituality would make him uncomfortable when he was illiterate. He never hesitated doing hard work of a coolie at the Yedshi railway station. He was accustomed to study at night. He served his guru Bapu Master to get elevated spiritually. He expressed his earnest reverence towards his gurus whenever their names were mentioned.

> ***He graced me with his pleasant glance,***
> ***And embraced me to put in trance.***
> ***It was Vitthal, my dear, my Lord,***
> ***To bless this devotee in full accord.***

In such words, he used to convey greatness of his gurus. He would call himself 'dust on saints' feet.' So, he was this much humble. It is said that the tree bows when laden with sweet and ripened fruits. Similar was Kaka's condition.

Kaka earned money by working very hard. However, he did not spend that money on himself or on his family needs. He reserved that money to buy books, for *Waris* and for staying and studying at Pandharpur during the *Chaturmas.* He had an excellent collection of books which he read, reflected upon them and ingrained them in his life. If one goes through the list of books in his collection, most of them are unavailable now. Many scholars at present find it difficult to understand them. His collection included *the Four Vedas, the Dashopnishade, the Eighteen Puranas, gathas* of all saints, *the Vichar Sagar Rahasya, the Adwait Amogh, the Siddhant Bindu, the Amrutanubhav, the Anubhavamrut, the Brahma Sutra Sharir Bhashya* and so on. Moreover, he had made available evaluative writings of Shankaracharya and some other scholars. Apart from these books, Kaka used to do *parayanas* of select books repeatedly. It would be followed by his reflection, meditation, interpretation and finally assimilation.

Kaka paid a considerable attention to correct and grammatical use of language. He would not like his disciples' unclear and incorrect pronunciation while reading or reciting scriptures. He used to ask them to say repeatedly until they produced the correct version. Many learned people would view him with awe for his scholarship. His life had completely changed. The passage of his life was from ordinary to extraordinary and from customary to prodigious human being.

> *A warrior is judged by his battlefield test,*
> *And a holy man while at eternal rest.*

A streak of fear did not appear on his face though he sensed his approaching death. On the other hand, the feeling of contentment was found across his face. He had become so much one with his God Vitthal. We hardly noticed how he himself became a scripture while reading it.

Nature of Kaka's Accomplishments

Kaka was devoted to *bhajans* and *kirtans*. He became *the Brahma* through this devotion and perpetually relished divine knowledge.

> *Let's feast upon pleasure divine,*
> *Forever with saints and people fine.*

A true guru moulds his disciples through his speech, behaviour and writing. Kaka directly or indirectly showed direction to society through his speech and conduct. Kaka's disciples kept increasing because of his overall conduct. Among youngsters, he developed interest in *bhajan* and he clubbed them together. These people became proficient in singing *bhajans, bharud, gaulani,* etc. and even in playing the *mridanga.* As a result, people would appreciate these young boys trained by Kaka. Most of them were hardly educated or even illiterate, yet Kaka would ask them to memorise *abhangas* and select shlokas by rote. Some notable names of these young men were Bajirao Chothave, Sada Chothave, Dadarao Chothave, Anantrao Bhise, Kalyan Bhalekar and Sopan Bhalekar. Some prominent names from the Upper Kelewadi included Dattu Kele, Uddhav Danne, Birmal Kele, Krishna Kele, Rewan Kamble, Vishnu Kele, and Vitthal Kele. Besides these people, even some women used to participate in *bhajans* and would sing excellently. In this way, a sort of competitive spirit between the two Kelewadis developed gradually. These people brought a lot of reputation to our village as their participation in *dindi*s, *kirtans* and some *phads* was very noteworthy.

The Bhagavad Gita says that man should reach the peak of his deed only to surrender it to the almighty. By this very principle, Kaka shaped me. He disciplined me to devote myself to the cause of persistent education. He himself was fond of education which he could not get. He might have decided to fulfil his passion for education through me.

Kaka would ask me to visit Kelewadi occasionally. I could not do so as I would be busy in certain examinations at that time. He would never feel bad by thinking that his son did not come and they could not meet. Moreover, my engagement in those examinations would make him feel proud of me.

I was fond of *bhajans* during my childhood and youth. It was the time when Kaka used to ask me to concentrate on my studies and not on *bhajans*. He insisted me to complete education first. When my education was complete, he began persuading me about the importance of spiritual thoughts. He instructed me to meet Kisan Maharaj Sakhare to get explained *the Vichar Sagar Rahasya*. Kaka would say about me, "You are quite sharp. Therefore, you are capable to achieve spiritual knowledge early. I love you, trust you and I am proud of you. Yet you keep in mind that your education and degrees only mean to fill and stuff the belly. If you want absolute liberation, then read, read and only read books on spirituality. After reading, do contemplate and muse on them. The study of these books will lead you to emancipation."

The worldly education is for the belly and spiritual education for the soul. He obliquely shaped me through this suggestion.

Kaka: A Dedicated *Warkari*

Kaka's personality was thoroughly rural. He looked very sturdy as he wore a milk-white *pheta,* a white *sadara*, dhoti and a pair of *joda*. He used to put tika on the forehead and wore a *tulsi-mala*. His tranquil face would produce waves of serenity in the onlookers' mind. His face was very placid and gentle. People believed that they would settle their every doubt after meeting him. His upright behaviour, simple living and virtuous thinking altogether became the essence of his life. He remained untouched by evils including allurement, illusion, jealousy, lust, anger and so on. In him, there was a confluence of varied virtues such as sainthood, studiousness, constant dedication, integrity and perseverance. In addition to these qualities, he never crossed any sort of limits in his life.

I remember Kaka's daily routine since his early life. He would bathe with cold water early morning followed by puja of his beloved Vitthal. Then he would water the basil plant and read the fifteenth chapter of *the Bhagavad Gita*. Besides, he would read *the Gita Stuti, the Dnyaneshwari* and Tukaram *Gatha*. He used to read loudly with clear pronunciation which made all of our siblings to memorise it. For so many years, he incessantly did *bhajan* and *kirtan* at night and *Kakda Aarti* in the morning. Besides, he would daily do *Jap*. Without break, he followed this routine till his last breath.

CHAPTER 6

Sandalwood Needs No Proclamation about its Smell

Sandalwood speaks not of his smell and even features,
Not only to trees but also to creepers.
The innate traits are seldom veiled,
Though restrained and oftimes nailed.

Sandalwood does not boast about its fragrance and tell other trees that it has got fragrance. Likewise, the inherent virtues do not require proclamation of their excellence. They involuntarily come out. Kaka had all the attributes of a saint. Along with self enlightenment, he even enlightened the lives of so many people. However, he never proclaimed about his deeds. Despite this, his fame unfurled itself. The common people attributed greatness to him. Nevertheless, leading sages like Kisan Maharaj Sakhare appreciated him for his greatness.

The impressions of some prominent people about Kaka have been included here. They, in fact, underline Kaka's actual image in society.

Righteousness of Numerous Births -
Kisan Maharaj Sakhare

Revered Kisan Maharaj Sakhare is known today as the most learned scholar in *Warkari* sect. This narration will be incomplete without the mention of an incident which took place in 1997. It happened in the Sakhare Maharaj's ashram at Alandi. The incident casts light on his opinion about Kaka. I was working at Chiplun at that time. To showcase Kaka's legacy or to propagate his thoughts, I had decided to prepare a collection of thirty-two Marathi saints' biographies. As per the plan, a book entitled 'Sant Vani' was to be published. I sincerely felt that the event of book release should be done at the hands of a sage. I could never meet Sakhare Maharaj though I had heard and read about him to a great extent. Kaka had done pilgrimage of North India along with him. So, I suggested Kaka to request him about the event of book release.

To meet Maharaj, we went to his *Sadhakashram* at Alandi. His saintly personality deeply impressed all of us. It was the time of *Kartiki Wari*. As it was the day of Dnyaneshwar Mauli's *Samadhi Sohala*, there was a queue in the ashram to have *darshan* of Maharaj. We all seated in the ashram. Kaka told Maharaj the reason of our visit. They had a brief interaction. Sakhare Maharaj said, "So he is your son! Does he wear *tulsi-mala*?" Kaka did not respond as yes or no but only gesticulated at him to say, "You yourself ask him."

Maharaj understood the implication and asked to bring a *tulsi-mala*. He said that he wanted to talk to me. I realized that he wanted to ask me the reason why I did not wear *tulsi-mala*. I therefore said instantly, "I was put on *tulsi-mala* by Kaka's guru Ramkrishnabhau around 1984. However, I could not understand its sanctity and seriousness at that age. So in 1991, I removed my *tulsi-mala* and began eating meat and even drinking. But I shall not do such things in future." Maharaj figured out what exactly I wanted to say.

"Forget your past and imagine that you are reborn now. I am putting *tulsi-mala* around your neck." Then he did so and applied some *bukka* on my forehead and there followed the chanting *"Pundalik var de Hari Vitthal."* I bowed down to Maharaj who instructed me to chant *the Haripath* daily and to do either *Ashadhi* or *Kartiki Wari*.

I realized that *tulsi-mala* symbolises prohibition against eating and drinking the unwholesome. Then Maharaj said pointing at Kaka, "Do you know who this person is. It is your *punya* of innumerable births that you are born to him. You have failed to understand him. But mark my words that every word uttered by him and every account of his life is worthy to be written in golden words. You write down anecdotes he has narrated. Send them to me if possible so that we shall serially publish them in our magazine 'Swasti Shree.'

Your father devotedly served Late Rangnath Maharaj Parbhanikar who blessed me." Then Kaka and Maharaj had some discussion on *the Adwait Amogh, the Brahma Sutra Sharir Bhashya* and some other books. Maharaj told, "These books are not easily available with common people. Only those who are great possess them." So this underlined my father's stature.

Maharaj assured Kaka in the words: "Now your son belongs to me. He has full right on me."

He was speaking seriously as my eyes flooded with tears which I could not stop. I, in fact, had no right to control them. Having understood Kaka's immensity, I was completely overwhelmed. Following Kaka's invitation, Sakhare Maharaj came to Chiplun. He released the book 'Sant Vani' which I edited. He even came to my home, blessed my family and endeared me permanently. He published 'Sant Vani' in his magazine 'Swasti Shree.' Whenever I visit Alandi during *Ashadhi* and *Kartiki Wari*, he gives me time though busy and fondly enlivens Kaka's memories.

Evidently Kaka is Mauli – Manoharbuwa Gosavi

On the third day following *Kartiki Ekadashi*, Dnyaneshwar Mauli's *Samadhi Sohala* takes place in Alandi. I visit Alandi on this occasion. Kaka himself instituted this practice which I still continue.

People would address Manoharbuwa Gosavi as 'Dada.' All the *Warkaris* stay in Manoharbuwa's *math* in Alandi and Pandharpur. Once I had visited Alandi during the *Samadhi Sohala* and lodged in the same *math*. I did not know what actually happened but Dada was telling other *Warkaris*, "Kaka is a dedicated *Warkari*. It is not easy to understand him. He is a great mahatma. It is not possible for common people to figure him out. Evidently Kaka is Dnyaneshwar Mauli incarnate." Dada himself was the patron of 'Maeechi *Dindi*' and had *mathas* at Alandi and Pandharpur. He was the vice-president of entire *dindi-sohala*. Kaka did Alandi-Pandharpur *Wari* in Dada's *dindi* for more than forty years. As a result, Kaka had close bond with Dada. Kaka considered him his own brother and would take his every care.

Kaka would tell us that very few mahatmas like Dada were left in this world. He advised that we should care for such great people. In the memory of Kaka, the first *Harinam Saptah* was held in Kelewadi following his demise. It was held opposite to the Ballav Rishi Shrine in the presence of Dada. He was present there with his family regardless of bad weather. Dada's presence underlined his affection for Kaka.

My respect for Kaka was strengthened when I came to know what people thought of him. Even my spiritual life was enhanced gradually.

Late Rangnath Maharaj Parbhanikar

It was the time when Rangnath Maharaj used to visit Yedshi and stay at Ramkrishnabhau Yedshikar for weeks. *Bhajans* and *kirtans* were daily scheduled. For his studies, Rangnath Maharaj would stay at Ramalinga hill for months. His *kirtans* would attract hundreds of people. It was the result of his melodious singing and impressive scholarship.

People called him *Guruji* whom they held in high esteem. Kaka used to maintain that *Guruji* had a great skill of making the difficult topic very simple. He would make even the commonest people understand any difficult topic with a range of fitting examples and illustrations whenever necessary. Kaka would also mention that *Guruji's* scholarly company used to be a feast during *Chaturmas* at Pandharpur. Kaka even served *Guruji* with utmost dedication.

Guruji rarely allowed people to approach him. However, Kaka was his favourite disciple. Kaka would scrub his body and bathe him. Kaka would look after his needs. In his company, Kaka picked up so many new things and even learned a lot. As a result, Kaka's mode of *kirtan* was influenced by *Guruji's* style.

Dhoot Maharaj brought out a series of books based on *Guruji's kirtans* and *pravachans*. Kaka had secured the treasure of Guruji's vocabulary. Kaka, therefore, never needed the above kind of books.

Guruji's contribution was very monumental in shaping Kaka. Probably that is why Sakhare Maharaj might have more affinity for Kaka. Like Kaka, even he was blessed by *Guruji*.

Bankatswami

Bankatswami was totally different person. He used to visit Yedshi frequently but would stay only at Ramalinga hill. He had a lot of affection for Yedshikar brothers. He was heading the holy seat of Neknoor which belongs to Beed district. While travelling from Neknoor to Pandharpur, his *dindi* would halt at Ramkund near our village. Kaka would solicit him to deliver a *kirtan* at Kelewadi. For so many years, Kaka did *kirtan* in this *dindi* during its stay at Ramkund. People of Kelewadi used to offer excellent breakfast to the *dindi*. Kaka began this practice which is continued even today.

Those people were very fortunate who came in contact with scholarly Bankatswami. Like Yedshikar brothers' love and affection for Kaka, Bankatswami's association played a monumental role in shaping him.

Dnyaneshwar Mauli Chakarwadikar

Dnyaneshwar Mauli was an eminent personality from Chakarwadi in Beed district. He was a devout follower of *Warkari* sect and had vibrant personality. He was a devotee of Hanuman. It will be more appropriate to state that Hanuman was pleased with his overall bearing. Mauli offered food to people on a large scale. This tradition is continued even today in his village Chakarwadi. Thousands of people visit this village for the *darshan* of Mauli's *samadhi* and have food offered there. He had achieved *siddhi* because of his austerities.

Close to our house, an idol of Hanuman was installed with a raised platform. It was done prior to my childhood. With the help of villagers, Kaka decided to build temple at the site. The temple reached its completion with people's contribution. It was decided to invite Dnyaneshwar Mauli Chakarwadikar for the installation of Hanuman idol in the newly built temple. Mauli would rarely visit other places for *kirtan*. However, he accepted the invitation because Kaka requested him and also because the program was about his beloved Hanuman. To give Mauli a grant welcome in Kelewadi, the streets were cleaned and decked with beautiful *rangolis*. People ritually welcomed him with the enunciation of Dnyanoba-Tukaram, with the resonance of cymbals and *mridanga* in *dindi*-cum procession. People were so overwhelmed to welcome Mauli, but he refused to have royal welcome. Following the *pranpratistha*, Mauli delivered *kirtan* which was so engaging. Nobody noticed how the two hours passed. Mauli said referring to Kaka, "Virtuous people are very rare nowadays. You have done this work which has no parallel. Your village shall have opulence permanently."

We had heard that Mauli had attained some *siddhis*. It was said that he delivered *kirtans* simultaneously at two different places. It was not clear what he thought about Kaka. They had a close bond with each other. Both of them were ardent followers of Hanuman. They propitiated Hanuman who indirectly gave them *darshan*. Even Bapu Master felt that Hanuman either dwelt in Kaka or accompanied him.

When the *kirtan* was over, people bowed before Mauli and he blessed them. Both Kaka and Mauli bowed before each other.

Mauli may have possibly come across Hanuman in Kaka.

The reason behind affinity between the two might be their bond with Hanuman. Mauli left our village after blessing Kaka and villagers. The fond memories of Kaka and Mauli are preserved in the form of temple.

Kaka: A Basil Plant Sprouted on Rubbish – Tatyasaheb Kore

Tatyasaheb Waskar Maharaj was from that family which had traditionally got the veena of Tukaram Maharaj. He was a spiritual authority. His disciples said that he called God's name which resulted in rains even in summer. Tatyasaheb Maharaj was from Washi. Therefore he was called as Waskar Maharaj. He had a lot of affection and respect about Kaka since he was from our neighbouring village. Many a time, he used to invite Kaka for *kirtans* along with *talkaris* from Kelewadi. Kaka's disciples would beautifully sing *abhangas* selected by Waskar Maharaj for his *kirtans*. As a result, Waskar Maharaj would appreciate them. He would say, "Kaka, you have groomed your people very well. Why do you join Manohardada's *dindi* though you can join ours?" Despite this suggestion, Kaka remained unchanged. *Bharuds* sung by the people of Kelewadi and their disguise remained quite popular.

Once, Waskar Maharaj's *kirtan* reached an interesting point. He referred to a shloka and wanted somebody to recite it. He asked all the people present there, "Who will cite the reference?" Everybody looked puzzled. Maharaj looked at Kaka, who, as per expectation, clearly articulated the shloka from *the Bhagavad Gita.*

Moved by the response, Maharaj said in front of thousands of people, "It is the most difficult shloka from fifth chapter of *the Bhagavad Gita.* What is the use of teaching to you? Haven't you seen the illiterate person? Kaka is a basil plant sprouted on rubbish. It is always sacred wherever it grows. Had he got conducive atmosphere and education, just imagine where he would have reached. May he expand his scholarship in Kelewadi. My blessings are with him forever."

Kaka: A Great Philanthropist – Bharat Chothave

Bharat Chothave is the son of Kaka's close associate Bajirao Chothave. About Kaka, Bharat states:

"Since my father was mostly in Kaka's company, I too was attached to Kaka. He was a dedicated *Warkari*. His main absorption was calling God's name and delivering *kirtan* which were the essence of *Warkari* sect.

Kaka led his family life which he shouldered as a responsibility. He dedicated every moment of his life to spiritual cause. Humility and simple living was the core of his life. He enlightened much orthodox Kelewadi and brought a lot of reputation to the village. In the words of Saint Tukaram:

> *Saints' life is for the world's gains,*
> *Who oblige us with their unbounded pains.*

The Vedas mention so many things but one needs to know their meaning. The principal concern of *the Vedas* is the advancement of the soul. Kaka had a virtuous mind and was miles away from envy. Bapu Master once had said that in Kaka one could find the aspects of Lord Hanuman. In his lifetime only, Kaka had gained that ability to have unification with the almighty.

However, Kaka did not stop only with this accomplishment. He did the revolutionary work of making positive changes in society. He shaped the lives of those whoever came in his contact; may they be labourers, college students or illiterate villagers. According to *the Vedas,* one should necessarily think about social advancement besides the soul. Like Tukaram Maharaj, Kaka was aware of it and therefore,

We know the Vedas, their meaning better;
Rest are to be laden by mere chatter.

He would claim this with confidence. It is hypocrisy to make a claim to have mastered *the Vedas* after just parroting some couplets. The spiritual authorities only like Saint Tukaram could understand the real meaning of *the Vedas.* This meaning pervades in their behaviour and people like Kaka become another Tukaram while singing his *abhangas.*

Kaka with Saint Balumama

Balumama was a *Warkari* saint from Adampur who belonged to the so called lower caste. By profession, he was a shepherd as he was from *Dhangar* community. It is believed that his sheep still wander across Maharashtra as they have no owner following his death. Balumama's followers from various places look after these sheep. People believe that they can yield more from their farm if these sheep graze in their standing crop.

Balumama's herd of sheep had arrived in Kelewadi in 2006 which brought a lot of festivities in the village. Kaka delivered *kirtan* in front of the herd and raptly danced in the procession. It really surprised people so much as they felt that

Balumama appeared in the form of Kaka. The villagers will never forget the way Kaka danced at the age of eighty-six.

Kaka: A Guiding Lighthouse – Bajirao Chothave

Bajirao Chothave was one of those disciples whom Kaka shaped by teaching him *bhajan*. He served Kaka to a great extent. Bajirao alias 'Bappa' would accompany Kaka as if a shadow wherever he went. Bappa shouldered the responsibilities of *dindi* when Kaka was unable to do it because of his age. Bappa would never get upset or angry though he faced Kaka's anger occasionally. Bappa did not avoid serving Kaka.

Kaka's *bhajan* companions from Kelewadi considered him a deity. Some prominent names included Sadashiv Chothave, Dadarao Chothave, Bapu Chothave, Sopan Bhalekar, Limbraj Chothave and Anantrao Bhise. May it be the construction of community ashram, the renovation of Maruti temple or the *bhandara* of Ballav Rishi, the entire village would respond to Kaka's appeal and the programs were a huge success.

People would enter the village by carrying their footwear in their hand during the recitation and illustration of *the Ramayana* in the temple. The villagers put on *tulsi-mala* at the hands of Kaka. All people distanced themselves from meat-eating and many addictions such as alcoholic drinks. It was the time when women could hardly get out of their houses. In such a conservative atmosphere, interest in *bhajan* was developed among women. Women's *bhajan* groups were prepared in such a way that they could compete with their male counterparts. The tradition of *bhajan* is continued even today. Bappa keeps telling that Kaka was behind all these reforms and none will be able to reach his stature in future.

Kaka: An Honest Human Being –
Shri. Arunojirao Deshmukh (Dada)

Late Sopankaka Kele was an honest and virtuous human being. For the people of Kelewadi, he was equal to a deity. There was a reason why people respected him so much. He was from a small village in Washi tehsil. He had proved through his conduct that people follow the path shown by such a person who has upright thinking and who is miles away from addictions. People from so many castes and communities including *Dhangar, Maratha, Muslim, Dalits,* etc. reside in Kelewadi. It is found today that adults, youngsters and even teenagers are getting spoiled due to various addictions such as wine, tobacco, gutkha and the habit of gambling. However, Kelewadi was associated with Kaka where his words were respected. He belonged to the *Warkari* sect and his thinking was quite upright. He wanted his people to behave virtuously. To do so, he adopted the path of *bhajan* and *kirtan* so as to imbibe values in them. So, he influenced people and laid the foundation of nobility. People not only maintained a safe distance from addictions and unethical behaviour but also embraced righteous principles.

Some people from Kelewadi have moved to Mumbai and Pune to earn their bread and butter. The impact of Late Kaka's thoughts and conduct is found on these people. Through their behaviour, these people are trying to treasure Kaka's legacy though they are living in cities. They never forget Kaka's ideals and the path he has shown to them. It is very difficult to find such people elsewhere.

Sopankaka was from a poor family. His dry land could hardly provide him an income to support his livelihood. As a result, he had to work on daily wages. However, he was incredible by nature. I would like to mention an incident here. Once, the government ordered an inquiry into the bogus work in the Irrigation Department. It was alleged that the contractor and the official had forged record of the work which was not actually done. An engineer from the Department had prepared bogus bills and documents and had procured money. The papers mentioned that a group of labourers led by Kaka had worked and their fake signatures and thumb impressions were taken. Some people had come to meet me during the investigation. They wanted Kaka's statement claiming that the work was done in his presence and he was the team leader. The amount was in some lakhs. I was well aware of Kaka's nature since his childhood. It was sure that Kaka would not do bogus work and he would never lie. I sent away those people and advised them not to expect Kaka's help in that matter. But these people met Kaka and tried to allure him with a large amount. But Kaka did not yield to them and offhandedly rebuffed the offer.

The following interaction took place at the time of investigation:

> Investigating officer: Baba (father), did you go to the dam to work there? (Kaka looked at the officer very calmly.)
>
> Investigating officer: You wear a *tulsi-mala*. You tell the truth in the name of your God Vitthal.
>
> Kaka: I never lie. I never had been to the work.
>
> Investigating officer: Correct! (He exclaimed while clapping his hand with another officer.)

The officer and contractor mentioned above came to me once again. They said, "Dada, he did as you told us." Having heard that, I was so happy and proud of Kaka. Once again the officer met Kaka and tried to tempt him. He also threatened him that he would crush him under his vehicle. Still Kaka remained undeterred. I was therefore proud of Kaka.

I remember Kaka as he was a virtuous and truthful person. His son has become an eminent officer after having completed his Electrical Engineering. It is my firm belief that it is the outcome of his father's virtuousness.

I pray to God that may every village give birth to people like Kaka. May the rural population become ethical, get rid of addictions and may Kaka bless us forever.

The idols of Vitthal and Rukmini were installed in the new temple. Since that day, Kaka began the tradition of celebrating the day as the birthday of Vitthal and Rukmini. This practice is continued even today.

Kaka produced so many disciples not only in Kelewadi but also across the Osmanabad district. The word 'Kaka' is fatherly to whole Kelewadi. Kaka was nothing but the other name for seasoned spirituality. His devotion for his beloved Vitthal was quite earnest. To state it in the words of Saint Tukaram –

> *May I live or may I die,*
> *For Him is my life and each sigh.*

Not in the Public Eye: Kaka an Uncommon Ascetic – Manoharbuwa Gosavi

Arjun asks Lord Krishna, "What are the attributes of an ascetic?" Lord Krishna replies to the question through a shloka. The following is its critique by Saint Dnyaneshwar:

Arjun said,

> *"Yes my Lord, my dear,"*
> *Then god responded in words clear.*
> *"At complete ease is our tongue,*
> *When sages' fame is being sung.*
> *People with their mind fair,*
> *I reside there for fullest care.*
> *Vairagya shall praise them ever,*
> *Though they are slept and conscious never."*

The mahatma was born in Kelewadi who had all these traits.

Along with Dnyaneshwar Maharaj's *palkhi*, Kaka did *Wari* in Chandrabhaga Maee *Dindi* for more than forty years. As a result, a bond between me and Kaka was further strengthened. He would always say that he would become reminiscent of Late Ramkrishnabhau whenever he listened to my *kirtan*. He would also say that he found Bhagwanbhau during my *bhajans*.

Once, Kaka was invited to Pune along with his *bhajan* group. It was a Vitthal temple where they were invited for a *Saptah* on the occasion of Janmashtami. As per the plan, Kaka's group held the *Saptah* which included usual *bhajans*, *kirtans*, *Kakda* and *the Haripath*. The organisers were so happy as they never experienced such an event in past. They gave Kaka some amount as honorarium though he declined to accept it. The amount started causing a lot of burden to Kaka. When he came to *Wari*, he asked me, "Dada, I want to build Vitthal-Rukmini temple in Kelewadi with the help of this money." Kelewadi did not have this temple. The plan of temple was finalised and a villager gave land. With people's help, a beautiful temple was built and the idols were ritually placed. At present, *bhajan, kirtan, Haripath, jagar* and *Kakda* are held in this temple.

As majority of population belonged to *Dhangar* community, animal slaughter was on a high scale. The occasion of marriage and other rituals such as *Gondhal-Jagran* and vows highly demanded animal sacrifice. More than two hundred animals were sacrificed every year. Kaka made an emotional appeal, "Kill me, not the innocent creatures." Kaka succeeded in stopping the animal sacrifice. One can find Late Kaka's *samadhi* near the temple of Birudev and Ballav Rishi on the highland of Kelewadi. His son had held *Harinam Saptah* on the occasion of his father's first death anniversary. Throughout the week, our whole family was present there for the event.

The Maeemath *Dindi* visits shrines of various saints every year. I had decided to organise *Saptahas* at those places. The plan actualised as the *Saptahas* have been held at the religious places including Alandi, Dehu, Ter, Paithan and Trimbakeshwar. Late Kaka was present throughout all the days of the *Saptahas.* He participated with more than hundred *bhajan* companions from Kelewadi. Kaka's companion Bajirao Chothave was his important aid. I had a critical health problem on the final day of the *Saptah* at Trimbakeshwar. On this day, I was delivering *Kalyache kirtan*. Suddenly I had acute pains in the chest. I fainted due to increase in blood sugar level. As a result, I was unable to utter even a single word. It might have been a cardiac arrest. I was not able to understand what happened next as I lost consciousness. All the people present there were so frightened. The atmosphere became dreadful suddenly. Kaka started calling the name of Nivruttinath. He howled and cried out, "You must take care of my Dada. You may receive a lot of service from him." In these words he pleaded. It was his incredible affection and love. I came to know all about Kaka when I regained my consciousness. I said, "Is there any soul as fortunate as mine whenever you are with me?"

Let me pass away musing on Him,
Taking Vitthal's name, without being grim.

Subsequently, I had to undergo the surgery of vertebra and was advised rest for some days. I could not guess what exactly Kaka had in his mind as he persuaded me to visit Kelewadi and stay there at least for a day. I had to leave with him in a jeep. Kaka had already given some instructions to his *bhajan* group. He had told them that I was an authority in the spiritual spheres and I owned a *phad*. He also said that I had esteemed *dindis* during the celebrations in connection with Tukaram Maharaj and Dnyaneshwar Mauli. Moreover, he told that my *dindis* on foot visited the shrines of various saints. He concluded by saying that we had a long tradition in terms of discharging our duties to God. The villagers had arranged *kirtan* in the night. I stayed in Kaka's house that night.

I woke up a little earlier in the morning. I found that Kaka alone was beautifully singing *Kakda bhajans*. Following bathing he had completed puja. I was so amazed to find that Kaka recited *the Vishnu Sahasranama* and the parts of *the Bhagavad Gita* very clearly and accurately. I was conferred on the title *Kavyatirth* after completing graduation in Sanskrit from the Bengal Association. After listening to Kaka's fluent Sanskrit, so many questions crowded in my mind. How could he have achieved such a command? Where might he have studied? From whom he received the lessons? When Kaka's puja was over, I asked him about the secret behind his elegant Sanskrit. He told me that he studied under the guidance of Late Ramkrishnabhau and Bhagwanbhau. The more surprising thing for me was Kaka's memory even at that age.

Bajiraobappa Chothave arrived there when I was about to begin bathing. He told me that he had brought a Moti soap and even scent for me. When I questioned him, he added that Kaka instructed him to do so. I asked Kaka if he used those things. Kaka replied negatively and told me that he liked to bring the things for me. Then he instructed Bajiraobappa to bathe me properly. I was unable to control my laughter. I asked him what exactly was there in his mind. He declared that his house was consecrated by my stay there. He told his wife to prepare delicious food for me. Kaka's wife was a helping hand for him. Following her husband's instructions, the cultured lady happily prepared the meal.

> *Her worship is her husband's care;*
> *His feelings are her dear affair.*
> *The rest are mad of only riches;*
> *They are not wives but mere witches.*
> *Her views are as per the husband's line;*
> *A true wife hails him as a person divine.*
> *Which results in her being well,*
> *And she reaches the stage to tell.*

Kaka's wife had all the features of a dedicated wife. As a result, their wedded life had perfect harmony.

Late Sopankaka had extreme respect, dedication and love for saintly people. He used to consult Kisan Maharaj Sakhare to satisfy his queries. He would display utmost respect for many sages who are no more at present. They included Bankatswami, Sudam Maharaj, The Yedshikar brothers, Rangnath Maharaj Parbhanikar, Dhunda Maharaj Deglurkar, Dharmashastri Chudamani, Panditpran Bhgawanshastri Dhararurkar, Eknath Maharaj Palsingankar and many others. Some living sages like Sopankaka Bedre Yedshikar, Eknath Maharaj Deglurkar, Ramhari Maharaj Neknoorkar, Mengde Maharaj Neknoorkar and some others were the subject of his veneration.

In terms of devotional life, Kaka's son Murhari is his successor. His knowledge of saint literature is quite excellent as I have read his articles and books. Finally, 'Life has reached its destination.' Although his organs declined functioning and there began suffering, Kaka entreated God in the words –

> *Let my body give me strength,*
> *My Lord Pandurang to a length.*
> *Not to care this mortal thing,*
> *But for divine and infinite spring.*

Since everything was favourable, Kaka's life became contented. His worldly life became fulfilled because of his capable son and fitting wife. Even his spiritual life attained satisfaction to elevate him to the status of a sage.

Kaka's health began deteriorating because of his old age. His son Murhari shifted him to Solapur for better treatment though Kaka protested. He refused to stay there in the hospital and asked to take him back to Kelewadi, the realm of his deeds. He wished to die there –

> *Let my body embrace dust,*
> *Where it spent lifetime just.*

He was obsessed with his almighty Lord Vitthal whose name he always kept calling.

> *This life falls short for being content;*
> *Grant me one more to a great extent.*
> *May I ask for the supreme route?*
> *To serve my God, my divine fruit.*
> *Since time eternal I am your slave,*
> *My Lord Vitthal, for you I crave.*
> *This is my wish and only yearning,*
> *To be your servant is the desire burning.*

With this supplication and articulating his endeared God's name, he passed away on the fourteenth day of *Krishna paksha* in the month of *Ashwin.* He merged into the four elements. It was the time of *Kartiki Wari* and Dnyaneshwar Mauli's *Samadhi Sohala.* On the twelfth day of *Krishna paksha* in *Kartik* month, a grand *dindi* began in Alandi and it marched to reach the Indrayani river. Late Kaka's ashes were immersed in the river. The river's greatness is described as in "Bones decay in water." The ritual took place in the presence of Kaka's entire family. Bhau Maharaj, Chandrakant Maharaj and many *Warkaris* were present in the *dindi.* It was a moving event which took place at the bank of Indrayani and in the vicinity of Dnyaneshwar Mauli.

I have put forward my fond memories with Late Kaka on the event of his first death anniversary. I conclude with the expectation that may Lord Vitthal keep Kaka close to Him and grant him everlasting divine bliss.

Kaka's Development in the Company of Prominent People

For a long time, Kaka got the company of great saints and sages. Many rivers come together to become a sea. Likewise Kaka had listened much to achieve prominence. He keenly observed other people's expertise in *bhajan* and *kirtan*, their method of learning, their attitude towards hard work so as to gain perfection. His sparse reading, scholarship and readiness for hard work made him think only of *the Bhagavad Gita* all the time. He was quite imposing about his knowledge and outlook. We grew in terms of age and body only. On the other hand, Kaka kept expanding his knowledge and the way of his thinking. We were aware of his greatness as he earned a lot of respect. But we were not capable to gauge his spiritual stature. Now, we are able to discern it but time has gone. The only thing left to us is to remember him and to follow the path he has shown.

I would not say that Kaka was fortunate though he himself carved his fortune. We are after all fortunate because we are born to him. Kaka garnered a lot of virtues in the company of saints and sages. His blessings will always be with us other than which there cannot be more riches in our life. We lacked nothing till now. In future too, we are sure to have the same condition. So it is the result of Kaka's righteousness.

How could be Murhari's condition after the assertion of his father's illustriousness by learned people? He would be overwhelmed because of his father's greatness and his respect towards him. Tears would have appeared in his eyes. Arjun came to know Krishna's immensity only after witnessing His *Vishwaroop Darshan* following which he responded, "O Lord Krishna! O Yadava! O my friend! I said this only because of my ignorance. I failed to measure your infiniteness." The similar would have been Murhari's condition.

Kaka adopted simple living and calmly chose the path of spirituality and illuminated people's lives by awakening them. Besides his *Waris* to Alandi, Dehu, Pandharpur, he went on pilgrimage to so many holy places in North India and Gujarat. With the help of *bhajan* and *kirtan*, he brought out changes in his own and surrounding area. Yet vanity could never touch him. The following description from the third chapter of *Dnyaneshwari* completely befits Kaka:

No desire can cheat him ever,
Even the baits very clever.
Though they are often water fenced,
Leaves of lotus are never drenched.
He seems close to one and all,
And looks like even big and small.
Though sun's image on water stays with it,
It's not like the sun even a bit.
If you view him in general sense,
He looks like commoners hence.
How to judge him perfectly fine,
As none can guess about his sign.
The person with these features prime,
Is far apart from every grime.
Of hope, desire and any lust,
He is the person you can trust.
He is the yogi and real sage,
The person rare at any stage.
You attain this state, I advise you,
Which is achieved by a very few.

CHAPTER 7

Kaka through the
Eyes of Suresh Londhe

Many students would come to
Barshi for their further education. Some of them had become my
friends. Suresh Londhe was my bosom friend who hailed from
Jeur in Solapur district. Once, I invited my friends to Kelewadi
during summer vacation. As per the plan, we all friends came
to Kelewadi. None of my friends had seen Kaka before. Suresh
Londhe has written his impressions about Kaka following his visit
to Kelewadi. He writes – "We reached Kelewadi in the evening.
After reaching there, I came to know that Murhari's father does
the intense hard work of digging wells for the livelihood of his
family. However, he never fails to provide money for Murhari's
education. I was moved to see his tireless hard work to educate
his son. Instantly it made me recall my parents. My father knows
nothing about me, for instance the class in which I am studying,

place of my stay in Barshi, the amount I need, the things I eat, etc. We have a joint family in which my uncle is the head of our family. I am provided maximum one thousand rupees a month.

Kaka's vision about his son's education made me feel proud of him. After visiting Kelewadi, my friendship compelled me to make a comparison. Murhari's sister gave us water. After drinking it, we sat on the platform of the temple. It was the time of nightfall. Slowly the streets began getting crowded and dusty due to cows and goats heading homeward. They were so eager to reach their destination as early as possible. Murhari left the place to bring mangoes for us from a certain place in the village. We were watching commuters on the street and waiting for Kaka to come. Actually we did not know Kaka, and even Murhari was not in the house. It was therefore impossible for us to recognise Kaka. So we were observing people heading towards Murhari's house. After a while, a well-built person came there who was carrying a rope which was tied to the cow that followed him. He was wearing a white *pheta*, a tailored *banyan* and a dhoti. He was wearing a *tulsi-mala* and had a tika of *ashtagandha-bukka*. We came to know that he was followed by a woman who was carrying on her head a bundle of firewood. After arriving at their home, they tied goats and the cow to their respective places. Then Murhari's sister gave them water. We could guess that the man was Murhari's father as Murhari's sister told him who we were. He came to us, greeted us and said, 'Did you have tea or milk? Then come. We will sit on the blanket inside the house. In the meantime, Murhari will arrive.' We did not eat mangoes as we already had taken milk. Murhari's mother Nani lighted fire in the hearth and began cooking.

Shivaji Kamble, another friend from Kelewadi was with us. He said, 'Let's have a stroll in the village,' and we followed him. He began telling us about Kaka – 'Kaka is a thoroughly holy person. He is quite straightforward and a man of determination. With the help of almanac, he instantly provides details such as the auspicious time to do something and even satisfies people's queries.'

After awhile, we came back to Murhari's house. Kaka enquired about us as if he already knew us. Then we were called for dinner. He insisted us for dining properly. At the same time, he talked on some issues including education. We realised that he did not know much about the field. Nevertheless, he was of the opinion that everybody should get proper education. He also expected that his children should acquire a fair amount of learning for which he was ready to undertake any sort of hardship. He told us, 'It is only education which is going to change your life. So you need to study a lot whole-heartedly.'

Kaka's maxim about learning completely changed our lives."

While narrating another experience Suresh Londhe records – "We had completed our dinner a few minutes earlier. Then arrived a man of Kaka's age. He was asking something to Kaka in a low voice. Kaka instantly replied quite loudly, 'Why not do it? We shall begin *bhajan* immediately as dinner is over.' We came to know about Kaka's resolute nature. The *bhajan* did not begin at once. The *pakhawaj* player was trying to tune his *pakhawaj* and the 'tuk-tuk' sound was heard.

A harmonium and some cymbals were brought there. Kaka was still making enquiries about our school, city and other related matters. He did not utter even a single word about Murhari's study and his son's overall conduct. We came to know how much he trusted his son. Then the *bhajan* began and we started feeling awkward. Kaka noticed it easily and instructed Murhari to take us to the raised platform of the temple. He perceived that *bhajan* was an uninteresting matter for us.

We came to the temple platform. After spreading the carpet, we began chatting. By that time, something else was going on in my mind. I realised one thing about rural people. These people are more humane and affectionate though they are illiterate and away from urban life. I even realised that our culture is firmly rooted in rural India. One more thing I figured out clearly – the difference between Murhari's father and mine. They are distinctly different though their names are similar as both of them are 'Kaka.' My father is highly educated whereas Sopankaka was barely literate; my father is an atheist while Kaka is highly spiritual; my father never trusts me though Kaka is ready to do anything for his children. My father is exactly opposite to Kaka. He is obstinate, dictatorial, irresponsible and unconcerned about his children's pleasure and pain. Murhari's father is the other name of God Himself. He is quite sensible towards his children who moulds and directs them properly. He is caretaking and does everything to inculcate values in his children. Moreover, he gives them individual freedom. He is completely humble though he is the master in the field of spirituality. In spite of his financial difficulties, he strives hard for his children's future. Murhari might be very fortunate to have born to a devoted person like Kaka. Following our dinner, we went to the temple platform for sleeping. Murhari's house did not have sufficient space to accommodate us. It was the house of merely seven sheets of tin.

I was so restless because so many thoughts caused turmoil in my mind. I was not able to sleep though my friends were in deep slumber.

The chirping of birds from the trees awakened me in the morning. We all got up. I was surprised to find that Kaka was sitting by me. He said while looking at me, 'You moved upward in your bed while you slept. I think you are habituated to move upward like this in your sleep. Your bed was left at your feet. I suppose you are not hurt.' I told him that I was not at all hurt. Kaka responded, 'I see. It is good to move upward during sleep. Such people always make progression in their life.' These words were uttered to me more than forty years ago. It was a kind of blessing for me. Today, I am quite happy because of Kaka's blessings.

This incident underlines that it is necessary to derive positive meaning from an event so as to encourage children for their better future.

We returned to Murhari's house. I was so lucky to watch Kaka doing his puja. He had so many books in his collection and had gone through them. I told my friends to get ready and come back after visiting Shivaji Kamble's house.

All of us sat there while Kaka was discussing about the work to be done on that day. Kaka told us, 'You will find so many mangoes on the tree in the upper farm. Below the tree, you may find the ripened fruits. So, do not dare to climb the tree.' In this way Kaka gave us the affectionate warning. He was smiling as he passed on his caution.

Kaka arrived when we were eating *bhakris*, mangoes and enjoying swimming. Somebody suggested us to head towards the place where Kaka and his companions were digging a well. To reach the location, we walked for one kilometre. The well was roughly twenty five feet deep and had no water. The labourers were hauling out the stones broken by dynamite. Kaka was making a hole with the help of an iron bar. The owner was inspecting the work from above. When Kaka saw us there, he asked, 'Have you had your lunch? Have you eaten mangoes?' He directed us to go the shed. We were told that a man and a woman earned twenty and fifteen rupees a day respectively. Kaka was interacting with us while passing on instructions about the work to his companion. His dedication towards his work was worthy of appreciation. Nani was handing over the buckets of earth to her work mates. I was shocked to find them working even in that searing heat. Their hard work made us more responsible towards our studies."

This is Suresh Londhe's impression about Kaka and our family though he stayed in Kelewadi only for twenty four hours. He has even mentioned how Kaka strived for social change. He writes, "In the evening, we tasted *aamras* and rested on the temple platform. At that time, Kaka called Murhari and gave him some money. Kaka told him to take us to Washi to watch a film. We decided to reach Washi on foot keeping in mind that we would be able to get a lot of mangoes during our way back to Kelewadi. On this route of six kilometres, there were so many mango trees. For me, walking at the time of night was not advisable though we could come back by a vehicle. But it was unanimously decided to walk and, as a result, I had to give in. We watched the film entitled 'The Burning Train.' Since it was a touring talkie, it had walls made of cloth. The sky itself was its canopy. I felt quite restless throughout the show as the thoughts of dark night clouded over my mind. It was highly impossible for me to walk in darkness. Finally, the film was over and we all began to walk. We could hardly see anything in that thick darkness. We could properly find out our way as we came away from artificial lights in Washi. After walking for some distance, we reached the mango groves. Murhari's friends from Kelewadi rushed to the mango trees to get the ripened fruits that had fallen below. We kept following those boys and did not notice how we finally reached Kelewadi. We had collected plenty of fruits. They tasted amazing as we gobbled them up. We found Kaka seated on the temple platform while reciting *abhangas* and shlokas. People belonging to the *bhajan* group had just left the place. I supposed that Kaka was waiting for our arrival. He told us to drink water before sleeping and turned to his bed. At this point, I realised that our journey on foot was a thrilling experience than by a jeep.

We woke up in the morning. All of us were thinking to go back to Barshi. Kaka was busy in his usual puja. Nani was insisting us to stay for one more day. When Kaka's puja was over, he said to all of us, 'Today you visit Kunthalgiri where you can get khoa of excellent quality. Just taste it and come back.' But we remained firm on our decision to return. Kaka told Murhari to bring some khoa from the place where it was prepared. When Murhari came back, Kaka packed khoa for each of us and told us to go carefully. He asked Murhari to leave us at a certain diversion and left for his daily work. As we left, I was tremendously influenced by Kaka.

Both Murhari and I studied in the same class up to our H. S. C., but for higher education we shifted to new locations. After the first visit, I could not go to meet Kaka even during my vacation. After the death of my friend's father, I happened to visit the village Pardi which is close to Kelewadi. So, with my friends I went to Kelewadi to meet Kaka. Suddenly he came and stood before me. I said, 'Have you recognised me Kaka?' Then he recalled my name and blessed me. He insisted, 'I will not let you go unless you have your meal here.' There had been some people with Kaka as usual even on that day. Somebody enquired, 'Who are these people?' Kaka replied, 'He is Murhari's bosom friend. He has come to meet me today after a long time. He has a mansion-like house and a huge farmland. Besides, he has a big business and a factory.'

While pointing at the image of Lakshmi on the calendar he said, 'You can see there the Lakshmi of his factory.' Kaka's appreciation knew no boundaries. An elderly person asked me, 'Is he your relative?' Kaka said 'No' to the man. Then the man asked me in surprise, 'Then how come he knows all these things about you?' I replied, 'We are not at all relatives. I belong to *Maratha* community whereas he is a *Dhangar*. However, our bond surpasses bold relationships.' The man did not wish to speak next. Since he was from Kaka's field of spirituality, they had interesting discussion. After enjoying Kaka's hospitality, we were about to depart when the man exclaimed, 'Undoubtedly, Kaka is such a mahatma who is thoroughly spiritual.'

Once again it underlined Kaka's greatness.

In this way, I could meet Kaka occasionally. He always wanted me to stay there with him a little longer. Sometimes people would tell him about Murhari. He would respond to them in the words – 'May God grant him more wisdom. What can I tell him? He may do whatever he finds to be good.'

Thus, Kaka advocated personal freedom. He was fond of farm land. He was so happy when Murhari decided to buy agricultural land. He would appreciate Murhari by referring to the farm while talking with certain businessman from Washi or with some other people. Kaka used to do intense hard work in the farm. He would stay there for hours. His desire to work was still there though his health did not allow him to do so. In spite of his old age, he was always vigorous.

Once Kaka expressed his desire of cultivating pomegranate in his farm. This new task involved some difficulties related to pomegranate seedlings, drip irrigation, etc. So the frequency of my visits to Murhari's farm increased. Whenever I visited the farm, I found Kaka getting some works done from his people. He would keep saying, 'I wish to write down about my services to my gurus. Both Murhari and you give me time to do so.' Once I said 'Yes' to him but Murhari failed to get time. Recently, Kaka's health was not doing well. But he used to visit Washi on the day of weekly bazaar. He would prefer walking to Washi and back to Kelewadi. He never discontinued this routine. On occasions, we would request him as 'You go to Murhari to stay with him in the city.' He would respond to this suggestion in the words, 'No, I feel comfortable only in Kelewadi. How can Tanaji handle works in the farm?' Kaka's concern and care about Tanaji would increase whenever he was away from Kelewadi. So, Kaka's primary regard was others' pleasure and pains.

'This year I want to visit Pandharpur on *Kartiki Ekadashi*. Ask Murhari to come with his car', Kaka expressed his desire. I responded to him affirmatively. When I visited Mumbai, Murhari gave me Kaka's hearing machine for its repair. After a lot of search, I got it repaired. Generally Kaka did not like to put the machine to his ear. He would prefer to use it only during Murhari's presence as he would pay a lot of attention to his father. Besides, he would use it just to avoid Murhari's disapproval when he doesn't use it. Kaka was quite affectionate towards Tanaji for whom he always cared. He would point out shortcomings in Tanaji's work whenever necessary. However, he never interfered in Tanaji's work. It was against his nature to go poking his nose into other people's business.

Once it was a little late to reap the crop of gram and wheat due to labour shortage. Kaka executed the work at that time and the schedule of his meals consequently affected his health. Mosquitoes and change in drinking water caused some trouble to Kaka's health. So, once he felt dizzy and fell down. Tanaji hospitalized him and brought him back to Kelewadi on the following day after giving him saline and some medicine. Kaka resumed his works after some days. Accordingly, Kaka's health deteriorated and he became weaker and weaker day by day. One day he became unconscious. So Tanaji hospitalised him once again. Doctors diagnosed a problem in Kaka's kidney and he was shifted to Osmanabad. There had been a minor improvement in his health as he started responding to medicines. Murhari shifted him to Solapur as doctors advised to do so for better treatment. Kaka strongly desired to read *the Bhagavad Gita* and other scriptures though he could not because of his saline.

Kaka's Preoccupation with Reading

During Kaka's hospitalisation, Murhari sneezed and wiped his nose. Kaka called me towards him and told me to ask Murhari to take a pill. Although Kaka was seriously ill, he kept saying, 'I am absolutely okay. It is *Ekadashi* today and very soon there will be Diwali. We shall celebrate Diwali by calling our people together.' Every day he would count the day and mention the day of Diwali. During his hospitalisation, Kaka felt extremely uncomfortable. He would forcefully remove the saline and masks though doctors made every attempt to make him feel comfortable. Finally doctors advised us to put him on ventilation. We realised that Kaka's health was worsening further. We could not endure Kaka's suffering. He wanted to speak a lot but he could not. Murhari's wife Manisha and their children were called from Mumbai. Kaka recognised them and gesticulated. So this much was his interaction. He was unable to bear his own predicament. Doctors told us – 'He is responding only because of the ventilation. His body has already stopped responding to medicines.' We were so helpless. Our mind was not ready to accept the truth which the doctors told. We hoped that Kaka would respond to medicine sooner or later. He expressed his final wish – 'Take me to Kelewadi.' So, all of us including Murhari and his kinsmen decided to take Kaka to Kelewadi. The ventilator was still functioning while bringing him back to Kelewadi. As a result, he survived till he was brought to the village. He stopped breathing as soon as the ventilator was removed."

When we came across such responses from people, it underscores how much respect Kaka earned. He never proclaimed about his deeds. In other words it was his feature to do away with propaganda. As Saint Tukaram says, sandalwood needs no proclamation of its fragrance. The rising sun awakes birds, humans and other beings. A cloud need not tell peacock to dance. It begins dancing as it spots cloud in the sky. A thing in mind can never be concealed.

> *The sun intends not people to awake,*
> *Nor his rays blink for anybody's sake.*
> *Clouds, says Tuka, appeal not peacocks to dance;*
> *Truth is never hidden even by chance.*

Likewise spread Kaka's fame.

CHAPTER 8

Thus Took Place Some Events

1. When is excellent a fruit's seed,
Sweet and juicy shall be its breed.

It happened around 1982-83. I was studying at Barshi in twelfth standard. I was staying in the government hostel. Saturday was the day of weekly bazaar. Merchants from neighbouring villages used to visit the bazaar to sell their commodities. From Kelewadi, my friend's brother Bhaskar Chothave had come to Barshi for the bazaar. He came to my hostel to meet me but could not find me there. I was not in my room as I had gone to watch a film with my friend Datta Sathe. After returning to Kelewadi, Bhaskar reported the matter to Kaka. The following interaction took place between them:

Kaka: How are you Bhaskar? Is everything okay with
    Murhari?

Bhaskar: I could not meet him.

Kaka: What? You could not meet him? Where had he
    gone?

Bhaskar: How could I know?

Kaka: You should have asked somebody regarding his
    whereabouts.

Bhaskar: I came to know from other boys that he had
    gone to watch a film.

Following this conversation, Kaka remained silent. He immediately sent me a letter:

"Dear Son Murhari,

Many blessings!

I have come to know that you watched a film. But I believe that it is not true. If it is true then it is not appropriate."

Watching film or *tamasha* was strictly prohibited in our family. As a result, Kaka seemed to have greatly pained.

I sent reply to the letter. I wrote, "I watched no film. I, in fact, never watch films. You trust others, not your son."

In this way I audaciously responded with fullest mendacity.

Having gone through my letter, Kaka wrote to me once again: "I fully trust my son. I was wrong to mistrust him. I am sure that my son would never behave in that way. As Saint Tukaram assures

> ***When is excellent a fruit's seed,***
> ***Sweet and juicy shall be its breed."***

The letter was exceedingly penetrating for me. It served to be eye opening throughout my life. I would have felt bad if Kaka had directly scolded me. However, it would not have made profound impact on my mind. Kaka's letter proved that one can win hearts by trust and love. The incident gave me a new direction and shaped my life. Since the event, I never dared to tell lies to Kaka.

The Bhagavad Gita says that one should strive for highest achievements only to offer them to God. In the same way, Kaka moulded me.

2. Your learning is merely a belly-filling stuff – Kaka

Kaka might have decided to educate me because he himself was passionate about education which he could not get. He used to intensely toil for educating me. Some people advised him to enrol my name in polytechnic. But he had a strong passion to educate me further. I, of course, fulfilled his expectations. I obtained good marks in H. S. C. and took admission in Electrical Engineering at Government Engineering College, Aurangabad. I completed my graduation and joined the Garware Company. While doing the job I completed M. B. M. in Marketing. It was followed by my posting in M. S. E. B. at Chiplun as a Junior Engineer. Without any gap, I subsequently completed six degree courses including M. I. E., L. L. B., D. I. T. and Journalism.

Occasionally, Kaka used to ask me to visit Kelewadi. I would tell him that I was busy in certain examinations. As a result, He would become happy and have sense of pride about me. However, he would strongly feel that I should even study spirituality. When I was a child, Kaka would advise me to concentrate on my studies instead of *bhajan*. The same Kaka now started convincing me to embrace the spiritual line of thoughts instead of continuing my further education. He wanted me to get lessons in certain spiritual books from Kisan

Maharaj Sakhare. Kaka asked me to begin with *the Vichar Sagar Rahasya*.

He would say, "You are very sharp. As a result you are capable to do it instantly." About me he had intense love, trust and pride.

He used to assert, "No matter of your ceaseless education and numerous degrees, your learning is merely a belly-filling stuff. It may provide you bread and butter and even a job. If you want to attain salvation, it is a must to construe spiritual books and to meditate and ruminate over them."

3. A Miracle during *Chaturmas*

When Kaka was at Yedshi he used to work as a coolie throughout the day. When his work was over, he would visit Bapu Master under whose guidance he began his spiritual education. He continued his learning also because even Bhagwanbhau supported him with whom he began visiting Ter, the shrine of Saint Gora Kumbhar every month.

Once Rangnath Maharaj Parbhanikar had arrived in Yedshi. He told Ramkrishnabhau that he had in mind to begin studying *the Vichar Sagar* during *Chaturmas* at Pandharpur. He declared that anybody desiring to join may do so. Kaka had a strong desire to join and he raised this matter to Ramkrishnabhau. Kaka's genuine difficulty was that he had no money to visit Pandharpur.

Following *Ashadhi Wari*, Ramkrishnabhau prepared to leave for Pandharpur for *Chaturmas*. When Bhau was about to leave, Kaka burst into tears. Bhau asked him –

Bhau: Why are you crying?
Kaka: I want to accompany you to Pandharpur.

> Bhau: It's alright. I shall take you to Pandharpur where you will get only accommodation. But everybody has to manage about food at his own cost. Nobody will get any sort of work there.
>
> Kaka: It's alright though there is no work. I left my home only for the sake of spirituality.

Kaka became restless because he was aware of his financial condition. He had no money to spend during his stay at Pandharpur. He was expected to stay there for four months without any earning. He had to call off his plan because he lacked even that much amount to spend on bus fare. He wanted to manage at least about the fare as he would adjust rest of the things after reaching there. The day of departure to Pandharpur arrived. People were expected to leave in the evening. Kaka got up early morning and began reading *the Dnyaneshwari* after bathing. Kaka's sister Mukta said, "Kaka, since a couple days you have been trying to get money for your *Wari*. But money is there in your book itself. You just find it out." Kaka flipped through the pages and found five currency notes of rupees two. He was sure that he had never put that money in the book. He understood its implication and thanked God for it. He was completely overwhelmed. He made preparation to leave for the *Wari*. As Saint Tukaram states –

4. **To the person of the purest heart,**
   God is near him and never apart.

Kaka went to Pandharpur. He attended *kirtan* on *Dashmi*. On *Dwadashi,* he began preparation to return though he did not want to do so as he wished to stay there till the end of

Chaturmas. But his financial condition did not allow him to stay. Bhagwanbhau knew Kaka's difficulty. He called Kaka and said, "You need not worry Kaka; the almighty is the caretaker who looks after his devotees. We need to be devoted to Him and let Him look after our worries. He will never let us down. As Saint Tukaram states-

> ***If you shed off every care,***
> ***God will look after each affair."***

Because of Bhagwanbhau's encouraging words, Kaka stayed in Pandharpur throughout the *Chaturmas.* Since then Kaka kept visiting Pandharpur with Bhagwanbhau every year during *Chaturmas.* He would selflessly serve Bhagwanbhau during this *Wari.* With him Kaka used to visit the Deglurkar *math* to listen to various scholars. For *Kartiki Wari* every year, Bhagwanbhau used to visit Pandharpur with Kaka, Sadashiv Chothave and the group of people doing *bhajan.* Like Pandharpur, they would also visit Ter for their annual *Wari.*

5. The Miracle of Veena

Once, Kaka had some disagreement with the young people of his *bhajan* group. As a result, he did not go for *Kakda* on the following morning. That temple had a veena which was put in its cover. The mellifluous notes of the veena were heard suddenly. People sleeping there thought that Kaka had begun *bhajan* early morning. They got up and were surprised to witness the miracle. The veena produced captivating notes of music though it was enveloped in its cover. The people went to Kaka and narrated him the incident. Kaka understood the unstated meaning and went to begin *Kakda bhajan.*

Nobody would hurt Kaka. For him the sound of cymbals and *mridanga* was everything. He firmly believed in the premise – "That person has all the riches who is absorbed in taking the name of God. However, such a person is rare." Kaka's daily routine was confined to this belief.

6. Kaka and Lord Hanuman: A Distinct Affiliation

Bapu Master was a moderate and studious person who taught Ramkrishnabhau and Bhagwanbhau. His spiritual stature brought to him the blessings of Lord Hanuman. Because of Kaka's devotion, Bapu Master would come across Hanuman dwelling in him or accompanying him. Two mysterious incidents need mention in connection with Bapu Master and Kaka.

During his stay at Yedshi, Kaka went to Bapu Master early morning on a Saturday. Kaka himself narrated this incident. He had a plan of heating water for Bapu Master and then going towards the well for bathing. The Master's ears were very sharp though he had no eyesight. The following conversation took place between them:

> Bapu Master: Who is it?
>
> Kaka: I am Sopan.
>
> Bapu Master: Why have you come so early? (He said it without looking at Kaka. Kaka looked around but found nobody.)
>
> Kaka: I am alone. There is nobody with me.
>
> Bapu Master: Hanuman is with you.
>
> Kaka: Which Hanuman?
>
> Bapu Master: Lord Hanuman, Anjani's son.

Kaka narrated the incident as – "I was shocked by the words as they were quite hair-raising. I felt to have given way to lightening. I only saw lightening and my hair stood on their end. Every year, we all used to visit Ter as *Wari*. Two *dindis* from Yedshi used to visit Ter as their annual *Wari*. So, one *dindi* belonged to Ramkrishnabhau and the other to Ramchandra Maharaj Bodhale. I was the mace-bearer in Ramkrishnabhau's *dindi* whereas my brother Sambhaji would blow horn in the other. The departure time of our *dindi* was around 9-10 in morning.

By this time, Bapu Master was not feeling well. I sincerely wanted to stay behind to look after him. However, I moved with the *dindi* heavy-heartedly. Our *dindi* halted at Jamalgaon which was at the distance of ten kilometres. I was absorbed in the thoughts of Bapu Master. As a result I hardly had any appetite. Food tasted bitter while dining. On the following day, a person arrived early in the morning with a message. He told Ramkrishnabhau, 'Bhau, Bapu Master's health has worsened. His condition is very serious.' When I heard the news I rushed to Ramkrishnabhau and said, 'Bhau, I will not come to *Wari* as I want to go back to Yedshi.' With Bhau's consent, we headed towards Yedshi. Bapu Master was on his death-bed and waiting for us to arrive. He sensed my arrival and said, 'O Lord Hanuman, I am waiting only for you.'

I said, 'I am Sopan. I have come back to meet you, leaving behind the *dindi*.' Master responded, 'Lord Hanuman accompanied you when you left with the *dindi*. Now he has returned with you to meet me. Now my life has attained fulfilment.' He died after uttering these words. It was such an incident for me worthy to be written in golden words."

Kaka was so overwhelmed while narrating the incident; tears gathered in his eyes. Kaka used to say, "Bapu *Guruji* was my adorable deity. He had lost his vision in the middle of his life. He made me drink the perpetual knowledge. I was a mere layman, a coolie who wanted to 'learn divinity.' I could show the path of salvation to many only because of his blessings. Is it a little thing?"

7. The Movement about Access to Dalits in Vitthal Temple: An Incident

It was the time when Dalits were not allowed to enter the Vitthal temple at Pandharpur. As a result, there began a movement against this prohibition. Some leaders planned to boost the movement with the help of *Warkaris*. With this help they decided to organize a *Saptah* which was to be chaired by Shrikrishnadas Lohia Maharaj. It was declared that every *Warkari* would be given *bundi laddo* as dessert during meal as well as a piece of dhoti. Since there was a shortage of people serving food, Lohia Maharaj requested Bhagwanbhau to send people from the Yedshikar *phad*. Bhagwanbhau conveyed his helplessness since his brother Ramkrishnabhau used to look after all the affairs of their *phad*. Ramkrishnabhau was not present there because he had left for a meeting. Both Lohia Maharaj and Yedshikar brothers were relatives. Lohia Maharaj said to Bhagwanbhau, "There is no problem though Ramkrishnabhau is not present now, but you send one hundred and fifty people to serve meal." In fact Bhagwanbhau wished to send his people but he considered doing so inappropriate without asking his brother. Some people asked Bhagwanbhau, "Bhau, may we go?" Then Bhau understood their feelings and said, "You may go but on your own responsibility. If Ramkrishnabhau questions you, then don't tell him my name." So, some people left to do the work. Bhagwanbhau said to the remaining people, "Even you may go. You need not worry as I shall convince Ramkrishnabhau." Following these assuring words, many people left except those who did not want to without Ramkrishnabhau's consent. Kaka was one of the few people who did not go. This incident underlines Kaka's discipline and obedient nature. Bhau returned from the meeting and came to know about the entire episode as he could find very few people present in the *math*. He was so enraged, though he did not express it. After a while all the people returned. Everybody was carrying a piece of dhoti in his hand. He said nothing to anybody but stopped speaking with them. Moreover, he did the same thing even with rest of the people from his *math*. He allowed nobody to approach him. Following this deadlock, all decided to go on fasting until Bhau opened his mouth. He gave way to his anger in the words "Without asking me they called my people to their place. Do they own my people?" Everybody begged Bhau's pardon. From the incident onwards, Bhau discontinued speaking to Lohia Maharaj. Both of them, in fact, were relatives of each other and the disciples of the same guru. After some days following the incident, Kaka invited Lohia Maharaj to Yedshi to deliver a *kirtan*. Bhau was sure that Lohia Maharaj would come to his house directly from the railway station. He therefore went upstairs and locked his room from inside. As expected, Lohia Maharaj straightaway went to Bhau and pleaded with him to open the door. Moreover, he broke down while pleading but Bhau did not budge. Consequently, Lohia Maharaj went back. Ramkrishnabhau never spoke to him throughout his life. Kaka used to give the account of the incident with a heavy heart.

Shri. Chakradhar Swami narrated an anecdote which is known as the anecdote of Sinderane. There was a certain king who lost his throne. After the incident, he left his kingdom. Then began the reign of the next king. Servants of the former king offered their services to the new. They began hailing their new master. However, Sinderane was an exception among these people. He was loyal only to his first master. He declined to serve his new master and even did not sing his praises. He had his own means of earning bread and butter. Years passed by and the earlier king acquired his crown and there resumed his rule. The same servants began eulogizing the king. He could not find Sinderane around and therefore enquired about him. He was reported that never ever Sinderane saluted the new master. The king summoned Sinderane back to the kingdom and honoured him for his loyalty. Besides, the king gave him half of his kingdom.

Kaka had the same sort of loyalty. He had ardent devotion for Lord Vitthal and he served his gurus with equal commitment. So many *Warkaris* went to serve meal without the permission of their guru and brought a dhoti as a gift. On the other hand, Kaka did not wish to do so and remained committed to his guru. As Hanuman was loyal to Lord Shriram, so was Kaka to Ramkrishnabhau. For the same reason, Bapu Master would have come across Hanuman in Kaka.

Kaka would advise to give highest prominence to loyalty in every field including the place where one is working. It was the time when Dalits were not allowed to enter temples. In this connection, there began a movement for opening the doors of temples for all people including Dalits. As a part of this movement, a *Harinam Saptah* was held with the participation of some *Warkaris*. Lohia Maharaj was the chief of this event. As noted earlier, Ramkrishnabhau was unavailable as he had left for a meeting. He was so perturbed finding that his people had gone to serve meal without his permission. As he was deeply hurt by the incident, he did not speak to Lohia Maharaj till the end of his life. It was not clear whether his ego was hurt because of the incident or he was upset about the movement supported by Lohia Maharaj. Thereafter, Kaka invited Lohia Maharaj during a *Harinam Saptah*. It means that Kaka implicitly supported the movement as he was against discrimination on the basis of caste. The tacit inference of the matter is that Kaka might be against barring Dalits to enter temples.

8. Your Father is a large-hearted person – Dr. Deshpande

Three years prior to his death, Kaka had felt giddy. He would not tell me about his health while speaking on phone. Occasionally, I would come to know about his illness; but he would insist me not to disclose the matter. At times, I used to visit Kelewadi. On such a visit, he started feeling giddy. I wanted to take him to a different hospital but he trusted Dr. Karanjkar only whose hospital was at Osmanabad at the distance of 58 kilometres from Kelewadi. So I took Kaka to the hospital. After Kaka's checkups, the doctor looked serious. He asked to do some necessary tests and suggested blood transfusion. Kaka consented only after protesting first. Accordingly a bag of blood was transfused which made him feel better. His shortness of breath also decreased.

After six months, Kaka had the similar illness. Then he was taken to the same hospital. The doctor told that the level of haemoglobin was quite low in Kaka's blood. I was at Thane at that time. I decided to take the advice of Dr. Gala who too was from Thane. I therefore asked my nephew to bring Kaka to Thane for proper diagnosis. Dr. Gala checked him and brought forward some stunning findings. He said, "Malaria infection is found in your father's blood because of which his haemoglobin is gradually coming down. Moreover, he has only one kidney. The other has dried up long back." I was awestruck by the findings.

All of us, including the doctor were quite surprised by the findings. It was miraculous that Kaka remained absolutely healthy up to the age of eighty-five even with a single kidney. In this condition, he always worked with the vigour of a young man.

The wonder, however, did not end here. Dr. Deshpande checked Kaka's heart and declared that it had swollen. At that age, it was difficult to bring its size to the normal level. The swelling affected the pumping of blood in Kaka's body. As a result, he frequently faced shortness of breath. The most likely reason behind this condition might be the lack of proper diet and intense hard work.

"How is the report of Kaka's heart?" I asked Dr. Deshpande. He quickly responded, "Your father is large-hearted." Kaka, in fact, was like the doctor's description. He was so magnanimous. His hearing was affected to some extent due to his age. He would very rarely use the hearing machine though he had one. When asked about it he used to say, "Why use it, to listen to worldly matters? Why should one do it? You speak to me only if it is significant." For him, the significant matters were difficulties concerning his reading, certain aspects from *the Puranas,* the memories of his *Waris* and similar issues close to him. He gave the least importance to the hearing aid which he hardly used.

9. I have seen my death, with my own eyes

This incident took place in 2006. It was the time of *Kartiki Wari* of Alandi. When the *Wari* was over, I prepared to leave for Mumbai. My cousin Dattuappa Kele lived at Mhetre Wadi near Pune. Kaka had been at Dattuappa's residence along with some other people. They had a lively discussion on certain topics. Nobody could know what exactly Kaka had in his mind when he asked, "Dattu, I want an *abhanga* by Dnyaneshwar from his *Gatha.*" Appa asked, "Which *abhanga?*" Kaka replied, "When fingers in the ears..." Appa opened the *Gatha,* searched for the *abhanga* and read it for Kaka. As the *abhanga* seemed quite profound, I took the *Gatha* in my hand and read it twice. It was read as –

> *When fingers in the ears cause no sound,*
> *Last nine days in your life are left around.*
> *When you try to see your eyebrows, but see none,*
> *Only left days in your life are seven.*
> *When nothing is reflected in your eyes,*
> *Five days after is your demise.*
> *When you can't see tip of your nose,*
> *The very same day your life shall close.*
> *This is sages' trait, as Dnyandev says,*
> *To think of release before some days.*

I read the *abhanga* repeatedly. I was so alarmed while thinking about why Kaka asked to open the particular *abhanga*. Tears thronged in my eyes and I came out of the house. I summoned Appa and said, "Appa! I am immensely frightened. Why has Kaka asked to open the specific *abhanga* though he knows many? What exactly he wants to suggest?" Appa tried to comfort me which failed to lessen my restlessness.

I brought Kaka to Thane in my friend's car though he wanted to go back to Kelewadi. I could not dare to ask him why he wished to open the *abhanga*.

It was not clear whether Kaka knew about his death well in advance. It is said that Dnyaneshwar Mauli's siblings requested time to grant one more year to their brother, and the request was granted. I believe that Kaka too was granted one more year following my unspoken wish. Kaka's implied manner of indication is not lesser than a mahatma's. How could baser creatures like us have discerned it?

Hardly after a year, Kaka left this mundane world and rested in the heavenly abode. He came to know about his death beforehand, but we failed to perceive it as we lacked that much spiritual stature.

I beheld my death with the eyes of mine,
The spectacle of which was grand and fine.
My joy was boundless, the worlds beyond,
To unite with Him, my Lord fond.

CHAPTER 9

The Reposed Departure

On 31st October 2007, I received Tanaji's missed call at 1.10 p. m. I could not call him back as I was busy in some work. After 15-10 minutes, Tanaji called me and informed that Kaka was not feeling well and therefore was admitted in government hospital at Washi. I was told that he had fever since the previous day. Besides, loose motions and vomiting added to his problems. Nani had gone to attend a ritual following the death of her sister's husband. There was nobody at home. On the first day itself, Kaka needed hospitalization but there was nobody to help Tanaji. On the following day, Tanaji brought my sister Nanduakka to Kelewadi and they both took Kaka to the hospital. After this, Tanaji called me. On the way to hospital, Kaka said, "It's of no use to hospitalize me. It's my time to say good-bye." These words were similar to the previous year's indication. From his words, I realized that his condition was much serious. I started taking necessary steps and began calling doctors of the Washi hospital. Dr. Galande was on leave whereas Dr. Mrs. Barate was available. I called her and asked to check Kaka thoroughly. After a detailed examination, it was told that Kaka had lost consciousness and his blood pressure was very low. I immediately told Tanaji to take Kaka to Dr. Karanjkar at Osmanabad as Kaka trusted the doctor. It was quarter past four by that time. I told them that even I would instantly leave for Osmanabad. Meanwhile, I called Dr. Karanjkar and told him that my nephew Tanaji would bring Kaka to the hospital. I came home and told my wife Manisha that soon I was about to leave. She wished to accompany me but I declined. I took Vivek with me and left. I got down and reached the H. D. F. C. ATM which was out of service due to power failure. In spite of that I left. I was not sure about the route to take up to reach Osmanabad. Finally, I decided to go via Pune. I left home approximately by 4.30 p. m. We had planned to cross Pune via Kondhwa and take up the Pune-Solapur Highway. We instead took up Saswad road and even drove for 20 kilometres. After realizing the mistake, we turned back to head towards the Solapur Highway. The fuel of my car was about to finish. Since I had a credit card, I reached the appropriate petrol pump. After filling the fuel, we sped to reach Osmanabad. From time to time, I kept in touch with Tanaji and the doctor. As we left Pune behind, Vivek slept in his seat.

I was told that Kaka's treatment began by 1 to 1.30 a. m., and there had been some signs of improvement in his health. However, he had not gained consciousness but begun responding positively to the medicines. The news comforted me. While driving I had to strain my eyes because of heavy rain, fatigue and the time of night. I wanted to rest a while, but my mind was not ready to do so. A little improvement in Kaka's health encouraged me to move forward.

We were not able to cross the distance speedily. On the way, I rested at Tembhurni for half an hour and at Jamgaon near Barshi for an hour. Finally, I reached Osmanabad at 6 a. m. I came across so many people in the hospital including Nani, Nanduakka, Sumitrabai, Mukta *mavshi*, Tanaji, Pintu and Narsing Bhalekar. Kaka broke down when he saw me. He believed that he was in Washi itself as he spoke, "I feel better now." He stated that the doctors from the hospital were very excellent like elsewhere as all of them had similar type of qualification. We cleared his misunderstanding by telling him that he was admitted in Dr. Karanjkar's hospital at Osmanabad. He smiled and admitted that he did not know about it.

After sending back all the people, Tanaji and I decided to stay with Kaka. Sumitrabai was with us in the hospital. The doctor had suggested giving liquid food to Kaka. We would, therefore, give him lentil curry and rice, milk-rice or milk-*bhakri*. On the first day, we had our meal at the place of our relative called Bandgar and left for Washi in the afternoon. Kaka's health showed improvement. He was able to speak clearly which unburdened me. For next two days, I stayed with Kaka. On Saturday, I told him that I wanted to go back to Thane. So, I came to Kelewadi and took with me some *jowar*, wheat, custard apples, khoa and prepared to leave for Thane. Initially, Kaka asked me to stay till his complete recovery. I told Kaka about my compelling responsibilities and requested him to allow me to go. Then he allowed me to go but on a condition; I had to meet him while returning to Thane.

Accordingly, I got up early in the morning and came to Osmanabad. I met Kaka. As he wished to bathe, I helped him get up and sit on the bed. Suddenly he started feeling uncomfortable in such a manner as if he had fits. He made strange movements of the eyes and his legs became stiff. I rushed to the doctor who immediately came and settled the matter. He warned, "Do not raise him without our permission." Consequently, Kaka's bathing was cancelled. I too cancelled going back to Thane. The doctor told that Kaka's blood pressure remained normal only when he was given the medicine called Dopamine. The doctor added that his condition may worsen like just before if the medicine was stopped awhile. The doctor suggested to bathe Kaka on the following day. During his fit-like condition, Kaka had said, "Garland that portrait. Give a rupee to that lady." Accordingly, a rupee was given to the housekeeper lady. The following day the woman said with appreciation, "Why did the grandfather give me a rupee?" How could she know the reason behind the deed and the mahatma telling to do so? Later, she would have realized what exactly Kaka wanted to convey.

It might be due to his improved health, Kaka began talking as if an absolutely healthy person. He would interact with me and Tanaji. One day he saw many wrinkles on his hand and said while looking at me, "When will my hands look better?" I replied, "Kaka, your hands will become normal like before." He further asked, "Will they become like yours?" Then I responded, "Why not? They must." These words comforted him. Once again he asked, "Then what should be done?" "It is damn simple; I shall scrub your skin with turmeric powder and gram flour so as to remove dirt. Then your hands will look like mine" – my assurance. With these words, gladness spread across his face. The next day Kaka suffered from loose motions which suddenly worsened his condition. He said, "I want to go to toilet", and started throwing away his saline. He detested defecating on the bed. As he was feeling awkward, I took him to toilet. Only then he felt better. I could not know the source of this energy though he had become completely emaciated. It might have been his will power and nothing else. His saline was removed for only ten minutes which made no adverse impact on his health. Then he slept in his bed. From Wednesday to Monday, he was given saline through both the hands. The skin on his hands was pierced by syringes for a number of times. The urine drainage bags were put to him to collect his urine. This hospitalization was Kaka's first ever experience in his life. For him, lying inert in bed was quite agonizing. He would keep saying, "I am absolutely all right; take me to home." Even we would tell him to "Get well soon; so that we'd return to home." At that time, Dr. Gilbile used to supervise Kaka. Dr. Karanjkar and my classmate Dr. Shinde were in regular touch with Kaka. Dr. Shinde had been observing Kaka's condition and therefore advised me to take Kaka to a better hospital. In this connection, he had discussion with Dr. Karanjkar and Dr. Gilbile. Dr. Gilbile explained in detail that Kaka was suffering from 'Septicaemia.' He told that Kaka's kidney did not function well due to infection which affected the process of blood purification. Besides, his lungs too were infected, hampering the supply of oxygen. Its result was lowering blood pressure which was put under check by Dopamine medicine. We were advised to shift Kaka to a better place to undertake varied checkups of kidneys, heart, lungs and blood. The doctors told us to do this to ensure proper diagnosis and resulting medication. They mentioned that such facilities were available at Solapur.

We, therefore, decided to shift Kaka to Solapur at 7 p.m. Even Suresh Londhe arrived by the same time. I sent my sister Sumitrabai and her husband back to home. All of us including Suresh and Tanaji shifted Kaka to Solapur. But Kaka thought that he was being taken to Kelewadi. A streak of happiness was seen across his face. Actually Suresh told him so. I asked Suresh, "Why are you lying to him?" He instantly spoke out, "Why are you depriving him of his happiness?"

Kaka was seated in the front seat which was leaned back. Dopamine was still given through saline. Meanwhile, Dr. Shinde and his colleagues spoke to doctors at Solapur. We reached Ashwini Hospital at Solapur by 10 p.m. While getting down the car, Kaka asked, "Have we reached Kunthalgiri?" Suresh said "Yes" and added, "Here doctors will check you and then send you home." Even I had to conceal the fact. Till end, Kaka thought that he was in a hospital at Kunthalgiri. Once he said, "These people belong to the *Svetambara* sect of Jainism and they are non-violent." It showed that Kaka had sound knowledge of various religions. The hospital staff advised to undertake some tests but Kaka protested. He was admitted in the semi-ICU ward. His health did not improve which added to our worries. We were impatiently waiting for the doctor who was referred to by Osmanabad doctors. We expected something positive from these doctors. We were ready to do anything for improving Kaka's health. Since there had not been any significant development in his health, he was shifted to the ICU the following day. It was the unit where so many serious patients were admitted. Some different specialists were checking Kaka. As a result, our restlessness kept mounting. He was being checked and was put under observation of specialists including cardiologists, pulmonologists, nephrologists and general physicians. Their observations were being recorded.

Both Tanaji and I accompanied Kaka since the beginning of his hospitalization. Besides, Suresh Londhe was with us. He supported us whenever required till the end. So many relatives and other people would come to meet Kaka. He would speak to all these people as per his capacity. Somebody came to meet him who had brought the *bhaji* of fenugreek and some *bhakris*. I was feeding it to Kaka as he loved *bhakris*. While swallowing, he suddenly had chocking that made him very restless. His eyes looked very strange as if he was on the verge of death. His breathing had almost stopped. Doctors rushed to the place and inserted a tong into Kaka's throat. A particle of *bhaji* was removed from the passage of breathing. I faced the heat of doctor's anger. He said, "Without our permission do not feed him anything. If possible give him liquid food." The doctor was affectionate towards us as we belonged to Marathwada. It was difficult time for us.

Kaka did not feel comfortable in the hospital. He had the habit of reading books after bathing. He could neither bathe nor do puja in the hospital where he felt very restless. He had asked to bring a book from Kelewadi for his reading. Despite his physical condition, he kept reading and taking God's name with the help of rosary beads. This was the essence of his life. There are some people in this world who have their firm control over mind, brain and senses. Kaka was one such person.

Death stood before him

During his hospitalization in Solapur, Kaka insisted to go back to home. He would say, "I do not like to be under their control." Twice or thrice he asked about the day of *Ekadashi*. He could not remember the day due to his illness. Even I had forgotten time, day, date, etc. due to the difficult phase of my life. Once, Kaka asked the nurse about the day of upcoming *Ekadashi*. When she provided the details, he helplessly uttered, "So finally, I won't be able to go for *Wari* on this *Ekadashi*." It meant that he saw his imminent death.

Kaka had already told me one thing. He had said, "On the boundary of our farm, dig a deep pit and put me to *samadhi* there. It also confirmed that he already knew about his approaching death. Throughout that year, he reiterated the matter a number of times either directly or indirectly. However, he did not emphasize it.

His restlessness was increasing day by day. As a result, he was put on ventilation. I asked doctors about the overall status of Kaka's health. They told me that they had little hope of his survival. We were so helpless. Kaka repeated his wish to go back to Kelewadi. So we finally brought him to Kelewadi to fulfil his final wish. The tubes assisting him to breathe were still there in his nose. On the way to Kelewadi in the ambulance, he was trying to tell us something through certain gestures. Even his eyes wished to convey something. The tubes were removed from his nose and he breathed his last after ten minutes.

It was 6.30 in the evening. By nightfall, Kaka, the spiritual sun also ceased to be on 8th November 2007. The whole village sank in extreme grief. In the accompaniment of *dindi,* Kaka's body was brought to our farm. In the dead of same night, funeral rite was done. Finally, Kaka was put to eternal rest.

At the time of funeral, somebody howled heartbreakingly. An extemporizing poet composed a poem and mournfully recited it before people. The poem described that the village had become orphan following the death of its patron, Kaka.

Kaka was the sun. As the sun illuminates the horizons even while setting, similarly he lit our lives before heading towards his eternal abode.

On the tenth day after Kaka's death, Manoharbuwa Gosavi alias Dada personally came to Pandharpur for the ritual of committing the bones. In the presence of *dindi*s, Kaka's bones were even ritually immersed in the Indrayani river at the time of *Kartiki Wari* of Alandi. Kaka was very fortunate. For many years, he did *Wari* on foot to his favourite places such as Pandharpur and Alandi. Throughout his life, he had impassioned attraction of the river Chandrabhaga and Indrayani. In the same rivers, he reached the full circle of his life. He attained *moksha*; he reached liberation.

> **Not only to Pandharpur these Warkaris go,**
> **But they get liberated by doing so.**

At this moment, my hand was trembling. I was so overwhelmed. Saint Tukaram's *abhanga* flashed in my mind.

> **Let's say goodbye to one and all,**
> **As we have received our final call.**
> **This is the last time we can greet;**
> **Thereafter we shall never meet.**

On the occasion of Kaka's death anniversary, a *Harinam Saptah* is held at Kelewadi every year. It is organized with the help of many villagers and Kaka's disciples. I pray to Lord Vitthal to let us continue the *Saptah* permanently.

Undoubtedly, Kaka's blessings are with us all the time. He hasn't left us; he will never leave us. He is always with us. He is, therefore, immortal.

As *the Bhagavad Gita* says – Weapons cannot cut, fire cannot burn, water cannot wet, and wind cannot dry this soul. As a result, it is always immortal.

CHAPTER 10

Kaka: An Epoch-making Person from Kelewadi

Kaka was born in a nomad *Dhangar* family which was in the darkness of superstition, illiteracy and ignorance. Like Saint Tukaram, he enlightened his people and elevated them from the age-old darkness. He was an epoch-making person from the precincts of Kelewadi. He brought out miraculous changes in this area. It was the place where local village deities were being worshipped. This type of worship is not called as the worship of God. As Saint Tukaram says,

Neither Jakhai Jokhai
Nor mother Mesabai
Mighty Pandurang is the God of gods,
Whom every soul always lauds.

> ***Randi Chandi claim such a right,***
> ***To drink wine and meat to bite.***
> ***Bahirao, Khanderao are gods akin,***
> ***Whom people feed and want to win.***

Khandoba was Kaka's family God. However, he renounced such gods and embraced the *Warkari* sect. He devoted himself to Lord Vitthal who is the deity of whole Maharashtra. It was told that Saint Narhari Sonar clasped the feet of Lord Vitthal and became unconscious for three days. Nobody could loosen his grip. So, there arrived his fellow Nivruttinath. He cast a spell on some water and gave it to Narhari. After drinking the water, Narhari immediately regained his consciousness. Then Nivruttinath gave him the teachings of *Warkari* sect "You can easily achieve your divine goal through the way of devotion instead of arduous asceticism and yogic practices. The *Warkari* sect is open to all those devotees belonging to familial life.'

In Hinduism, there have been some sects across Maharashtra including the *Mahanubhav, Datta, Samarth* and *Warkari*. The *Warkari* sect, however, is the most widespread and popular. Kaka earnestly made efforts to expand this sect. He built a Vitthal temple in such a village which hardly had any *Warkaris*. He worshipped his dear God Vitthal through *bhajans* and *kirtans*. The practice initiated by him still continues today.

Superstition was the subject of Saint Tukaram's censure. Kaka could not do this as he did not compose *abhangas*. The superstitious practices were put to end as he was the ardent follower of Saint Tukaram. He brought about such changes in his village with the help of spiritual teachings and behaving accordingly. It was the village in which there had been the prevalence of animal sacrifice and meat-eating on the occasion of wedding. All such practices have almost stopped as people have adopted the virtuous path shown by *bhajans* and *kirtans*.

Kaka's scientific temperament played a crucial role to eradicate superstition. People would consult exorcists to cure their diseases as they trusted superstitious customs. On the other hand, Kaka was against such practices. He fully trusted doctors to remedy all sorts of ailments. Because of Kaka's growing influence, people's superstition ebbed and they began entrusting health sciences for their better health.

Everybody has a certain type of hobby. Some people have the hobby of betting; some are indulged in gambling; and some make efforts of raising money through lottery. Some people are hooked to alcohol, and some are addicted to bidis and cigarettes. Such people feel bored when they are away from their hobby or addiction. Many a time, such an obsession is responsible for their downfall. Today youngsters are getting attracted towards addiction though they are aware of its negative sides. The hobbies such as reading, *bhajan, kirtan* ennoble our life. However, youngsters are not attracted towards such positive hobbies whereas they have strong fascination of destructive habits and hobbies.

Kaka's specialities lay in the way he brought transformation in Kelewadi. He de-addicted so many youths not only from Kelewadi but even from the nearby villages and created in them a lot of involvement towards *bhajan* and *kirtan*. Resultantly, these young men took interest in participating in *dindis* so as to do *Wari* on foot. So Kaka made these surprising changes in society.

'You will live, only if you read' was Kaka's advice to youngsters. He enlightened himself but even strived for social advancement. It is our family from where the upright line of thoughts is initiated. Mahatma Jyotiba Phule initially sowed the seed of social change in his family as he himself educated his wife Savitribai first. He opened the first school for girls in India in 1848. Savitribai was the first teacher in his school. Even Kaka was committed to give education to his children.

Kaka always insisted me for education. It was Kaka's urge which made me achieve eight degrees of varied fields. Besides his family, he enlightened society. He would advise my friend Suresh Londhe in the words – "Get excellent education. It's only education that makes you capable to survive." When Kaka began *bhajans* in Kelewadi, he attracted so many young boys towards him. Most of these people were illiterate. Kaka himself introduced letters to these youngsters and made them literate. So they began reading books. In this way Kaka helped building a powerful society through his own literacy mission.

Kaka believed that spiritual knowledge does not oppose worldly learning. He was of the opinion that worldly education is to earn our bread and butter whereas spiritual scholarship is for the elevation of our soul.

Through his actual conduct and *kirtans*, Kaka emphasized a need to foster good character. He dissuaded me from watching films. For the same reason, I did not watch the orchestra called 'Star Nights.' Instead, I studied hard that night and secured out of marks in Maths test held on the following day.

Kaka was the role model having all the features of an ideal father. Besides having a passion to educate his son, he ceaselessly toiled to do so. He offered a lot of affection to his son Murhari and his friends. He was a loving father who trusted his son and was aware of his pleasure and pain.

Kaka must have gained some mystical power as his extempore statements proved to be real in future. This power might be the outcome of his spirituality, his service to his gurus and his utmost devotion. Many people had witnessed his mystical power. As a result, people would come to him to resolve their problems. Kaka would clear their every doubt. He would use his reason while clearing people's doubts and even while advising them. He would never disclose the name of culprits so as to ensure peace and harmony among people.

Kaka's behaviour was strengthened by his balanced reasoning. It was his decree that his son should not watch films. He expected that his son's studies should not be affected due to unnecessary attraction of films. He, however, was not against watching films as a fun but only occasionally. He knew that youngsters are fond of films. For the same reason, once he had given us money to watch a film when my friends had visited Kelewadi.

Kaka was the true devotee of Lord Vishnu. Saint Tukaram describes the qualities of such devotees –

We, the followers of Vishnu, our dear Lord,
Are mellower than wax and boundlessly hard.

Kaka was very humble. He was softer than wax though he would become resilient according to the situation.

This incident took place after Sumitra's marriage. As per the usual customs, Kaka brought clothes to her husband. It was not a custom to offer a golden ring to the son-in-law. Yet Sumitra's husband wanted it and began sulking to get it. Kaka asked him, "Will you accept these clothes or not?" The latter remained silent. So Kaka packed the clothes to return them to the shop. He said while leaving, "You will neither get clothes nor your wife." Sumitra's husband was so frightened as he immediately returned to his village.

It was Kaka's strategy to respect the just and oppose the unfair and unjust. Nowadays corruption is so rampant in many fields. It has become a usual practice now. Thinkers are so worried about this menace. If people like Kaka are born in great number, it would help us fight and eradicate corruption.

Some officers from the Irrigation Department went to the Deshmukh of Washi. They wanted Kaka's signature on some forged documents of some work which was not actually undertaken. Kaka could have got fifty thousand rupees from them. But the Deshmukh was sure that Kaka would not do corrupt practices and sent away those officers. The officers directly went to Kaka and tried to allure him. He offhandedly rejected the offer. Today, there are numerous examples of people doing corrupt and unethical practices to own bungalows and expensive cars. Keeping in mind how Kaka declined the offer, upcoming generations can serve our nation and contribute to the national interests. The moral of this incident is that one needs to think beyond personal interests to do away with corruption. Moreover, our society and nation should be our highest priority.

Loyalty is a prominent virtue. Politics at present has degenerated due to such people who change their parties only for personal gains. In any field including politics, loyalty is always rewarded. Who is said to be legendary person? It is he who brings forth such changes to shape a new epoch that never occurred in past. These changes will not be adequate until people approve them. Besides, new generation should follow the path cleared through changes. Kaka made his people accept and approve *bhajan, kirtan*, vegetarianism and divine adherence to Lord Vitthal. Kaka's legacy is in continuum even today. Even in coming future, it will certainly be continued as it is firmly rooted in the soil of Kelewadi.

Kaka had sensed his approaching death during *Kartiki Wari* at Alandi. He just signalled it without making it clear. In the final year of his life, he prepared the record of his financial activities. He recorded all the calculations since the beginning of *bhajans* in Kelewadi. The record included expenses on the purchase of cymbals, *mridanga*s, harmoniums, etc. and contribution collected from people while building Vitthal Temple. Additionally, he prepared the record of expenses concerning the construction of our house, calculations related to farming and the list of total books in his collection. This confirms the fact that Kaka anticipated his advancing death ahead of time.

Finally, he wrote – "With the blessings of sages, I Sopankaka Aaba Kelewadikar, the humble adherent of my gurus Ramkrishnabhau and Bhagwanbhau state –

> *He graced me with his pleasant glance,*
> *And embraced me to put in trance.*
> *It was Vitthal, my dear, my Lord,*
> *To bless this devotee in full accord.*

After my death, the practice of *bhajan* in Kelewadi be continued. Nobody shall commit any sort of offensive act in the Vitthal-Rukmini temple. Moreover, no person shall be prevented from doing *bhajan* in it because –

> *One and all have the right same,*
> *To get moksha by taking Hari's name.*"

Like Tukaram Maharaj after whom Dehu is known today, Kaka brought a lot of reputation across Maharashtra to much neglected Kelewadi. This contribution of Kaka has made him the epoch-maker of Kelewadi and its surrounding.

GLOSSARY

Aamras – mango juice

Abhanga – a poetic composition especially by Hindu saint
poets

Ashadhi Wari – pilgrimage to Pandharpur in the fourth
month i. e. Ashadh in Hindu lunar calendar

Ashtagandha – a tika mark put on the forehead

Ashwin – the seventh month in Hindu lunar Calendar

Banyan – vest

Barbada – a type of grass seed

Bhajan – a devotional son

Bhaji – subji

Bhakri – an eatable made from jowar flour, roti

Bhakti – devotion

Bhandara – a feast

Bharud – a kind of saint poetry

Bhau –brother

Bukka – black tika

Chal – series of singing abhanga

Chaturmas– the holy period of four months

Chopdar– mace-bearer

Daate Panchang – an almanac

Darshan – visualising the deity/divine

Dashmi – tenth day of a fortnight

Dhangar – a nomadic tribe from Maharashtra, shepherd

Dindi – a group of devotees heading on foot towards pilgrimage

Dindi sohala – dindis to Alandi and Pandharpur

Dnyaneshwari – Saint Dnyaneshwar's rendering of the Bhagavad Gita into Marathi

Dwadashi – the twelfth day of a fortnight

Gan – division of the twenty seven Nakshtras

Gatha – anthology of abhangas

Gaulani – abhangas related to Lord Krishna

Gobrya – chubby-cheeked

Gondhal-Jagran– a performance to propitiate God Khandoba

Gopichandan – a type of rocklike substance from which white tika is prepared

Guruji – teacher

Hadpi – a kind of sack

Haribhakt Paraayan – The title used with kirtankars meaning exalted, sublime, elevated, lofty, etc.

Harinam Saptah – weeklong devotional program

Jagar – a type of bhajan beginning late night

Jamadagni – one of seven great Rishis

Jap – repeating and muttering god's name with the help of rosary/prayer beads

Joda – leather boots

Jogwa – alms in the form of flour or food asked by the worshiper of a goddess

Kakda Aarti – early morning bhajan

Kalyache – concluding

Kartiki Ekadashi – the eleventh day in a fortnight of Kartik month in Hindu lunar Calendar

Keli – an earthen pot

Kirtan – a devotional speech involving singing of abhangas in the accompaniment of mridanga, cymbals and the veena

Kirtankar – a person delivering kirtan

Krishna paksha – dark lunar fortnight

Kulswamini – family goddess

Kumkum – a red pigment used by Hindu women to make a round mark on the forehead

Lali – a lady with reddish complexion

Maharaj – a general term used in Warkari sect meaning a kirtankar

Math – a monastery-like residence at the places like Alandi and Pandharpur where Warkaris stay during their Waris

Mauli – mother, the term used for a kind-hearted person/Saint Dnyaneshwar

Mavshi – maternal aunt

Moksha – liberation

Mridanga – a musical instrument

Mridanga Mani – the ace player of mridanga

Mukti – liberation

Naadi – lunar asterism

Nakshtra – lunar mansion

Pakhawaj – mridanga

Pakhawaje/ pakhawajwadak – pakhawaj / mridanga player

Palkhi – palanquin

Panchang – almanac

Parayan – reading of scriptures on daily basis for a fixed period

Pasaydan – Saint Dnyaneshwar's supplication to God for the welfare of all humanity

Phad – The place under the control of a kirtankar in Pandharpur/Alandi where Warkaris assemble for their Wari

Pheta – turban

Prakrit – vernacular dialect

Pranpratistha – the rite of bringing life into an idol

Pravachan – religious discourse, sermon

Pravachankar – a person delivering pravachan

Pundalik var de Hari Vitthal – a chanting of Lord Vitthal's name in unison

Punya – righteousness

Rangolis – pattern created in courtyard/ in front of doors with material such as coloured rice, dry flour, coloured sand or flower petals

Rishi/muni – sage

Sadara – a shirt

Samadhi – shrine/tomb/the state of consciousness induced by complete meditation

Samadhi Sohala – a celebration to commemorate the day on which Saint Dnyaneshwar had taken samadhi

Sankranti – A Hindu festival

Seeing a girl – A ritual in which a would be groom and his people visit the place of a would be bride to know how she looks like, to know more about her background, her family, etc. before finalizing the marriage.

Siddhi – mystical power

Sukdi – powdery eatable made from maize and sugar

Taalkaris – people contributing to the kirtan or bhajan by playing cymbals

Taluka – a subdivision of a district, tehsil

Tamasha – a performance involving singing and dancing

Teel-gul – sesame and jaggery

The Haripath – collection of Saint Dnyaneshwar's abhangas

Tulsi-mala – beaded wreath made from basil plant

Vairagya – detachment, renunciation

Vishwaroop Darshan – the supreme/cosmic form of Lord Vishnu

Wadars – stone splitters

Wadi – hamlet

Wahini – sister-in-law

Wari – errand/trip, periodical pilgrimage in this book

Warkari - one of the Hindu sects in Maharashtra/a person doing Wari.